Images of God in the Old Testament

Images of God in the Old Testament

MARY E. MILLS

A Michael Glazier Book
THE LITURGICAL PRESS
Collegeville, Minnesota

A Michael Glazier Book published by The Liturgical Press

First published 1998

Published in United States of America, its dependencies and Canada by The Liturgical Press, Collegeville, Minnesota 56321.
Published in Great Britain by Cassell

1 2 3 4 5 6 7 8 9

Library of Congress Cataloging-in-Publication Data
Mills, Mary E.
    Image of God in the Old Testament / Mary E. Mills.
      p. cm.
    'A Michael Glazier book.'
    Includes bibliographical references.
    ISBN 0–8146–5935–7 (alk. paper)
    1. God—Biblical teaching.   2. Bible, O.T.—Theology.   I. Title.
BS1192.6.M625   1998
231—dc21   98–7582
                                                        CIP

Typeset by BookEns Limited, Royston, Herts.
Printed and bound in Great Britain by
Biddles Ltd, Guildford and King's Lynn

Contents

Preface

The title of this book reflects the approach which the book itself will adopt towards the presentation of God in the Old Testament. Most readers automatically think of God as a single figure, but the linking of God with the plural term 'images' prepares the way for the diversity of issues relating to the deity of the OT which will then be explored chapter by chapter. In the course of this investigation the concepts of unity and diversity will be held in tension with one another.

Much biblical language is metaphorical; God is described through word pictures rather than defined by a tightly controlled selection of words. A non-biblical phrase which both illustrates this use of language and relates to the purpose of the present book is 'flakes of glory' — a phrase drawn from a modern Christian hymn written by E. Taylor.

'Flakes of glory' conjures up images of a single reality, signified by 'glory', composed of many separate parts, the 'flakes'. God in the OT is said to have glory; in Ezekiel it is the Glory of the Lord which dwells in the Jerusalem Temple, for instance. This Glory is not defined in simple logic, in the OT, but is broadly outlined via visionary insights and much of its meaning is left for the reader to flesh out. The aim of this book is to show how that 'divine majesty' contains within it many different aspects, just as the rainbow radiance around the throne of God is composed of many individual colours.

I would like to acknowledge here the great debt I owe to A. Laing Brooks SHCJ, who has gallantly read her way through each chapter as it came into being and offered a wealth of helpful advice and support. I would also like to thank J. Clarke, who gave up important time to read through a whole draft of the book for me and who also offered helpful advice and encouragement. I offer gratitude also to Jayne Ringrose, who gave up time to research for me both poetry and manuscript illuminations which have furthered the theme of this book.

Timeline for the development of Old Testament traditions

Biblical time	Historical time
Creation	Pre-history. Defined by archaeologists as Stone Age and Bronze Age
Noah Abraham Moses	Egyptian records, but no reference to Moses
Joshua, Judges, 1, 2 Samuel (including Saul, David)	May be parts of Torah written under David and Solomon *c.* 1000 BCE
1, 2 Kings (Solomon and later kings) The two kingdoms of Israel and Judah (pre-exilic)	May be proverbial teaching, archives, psalms, some prophets *c.* 933 BCE
Invasions by Assyria / Babylon	Fall of Samaria 721 BCE Fall of Jerusalem 587 BCE
(Exile)	Jeremiah, Ezekiel, Second Isaiah
Persian period. Samaria and Yehud are provinces of the Empire (post-exilic)	Decree of Cyrus 538 BCE Ezra the scribe *c.* 400 BCE Beginnings of collection of Torah / Prophets may be at this time

Biblical time	Historical time
Hellenistic world	Alexander the Great 333 BCE First major writing time when books of OT as now known began to emerge
Judah is province caught between Egypt and Seleucid kings Maccabean revolt, independent Hasmonean kingdom	Daniel
Roman Palestine	Pompey invades Judaea 63 BCE First real library collection of a set of texts which would make up OT

1 *Introduction*

The title of this book may lead the reader to expect a systematic study of the God of the Old Testament (OT) — a biography of a single person, in fact.[1] Expecting a text of this sort, the reader might then say 'Are there not enough books already written on such a major topic?' Or perhaps the reader might say 'I thought that it was no longer believed to be useful to look for one over-arching theme or narrative by which to define the Old Testament'.

This book responds to both of these statements. First, it is not a book about an ultimate meaning given to a collection of different works when they were gathered together by an editor in the sixth century BCE or later. It will be relevant to refer to such an 'editorial God' from time to time, but the main focus will be on the many faces of the God of Israel to be discovered through reading about God in the separate parts of the Old Testament reference library. Each book in the collection has its vocabulary and structures of thought, its 'symbolic world', God is, in this sense, a character in each text and as such is presented differently each time. Much of the relevant research exists at present only in individual articles and monographs, dealing with particular biblical books or individual themes. The aim of the present writer is to put this research material side by side in a manner which enables students and other interested readers to explore the range of the subject.

Secondly, then, this is not a study with a single message. It is not A Theology, rather it reflects a plurality of theologies, present within Old Testament books. When these diverse aspects of the presentation of the deity are placed side by side it is possible to allow each to offer comment on the other. In this way the rich diversity of meaning of the phrase 'God of the Old Testament' can be revealed and the sometimes contradictory messages the reader of the Bible receives can be evaluated.

The Hebrew Bible is the product of several centuries of writing, to say nothing of the generations of verbal traditions which may have existed prior to a literary collection. It is likely that the books of the Hebrew Bible were not produced in their present format before the sixth to fourth centuries BCE. This means that the books involved emerged individually within the period of Persian rule of Palestine, the product of a literary upper class of society within the province of Yehud or Judah. The move from independent texts to a collection of linked works probably took place gradually within the time of the Hellenistic rulers who took over the province when Alexander of Greece defeated the Persians.

The final shift from collection to acknowledged resource books for a particular culture and religion probably occurred during the time when Judah was, briefly, an independent state under Hasmonean rulers, before Rome conquered the area and imposed on it its own regional structures.[2] The creation of a canon, a fixed number of selected books, and the development of a critique of these works in the light of ongoing cultural and religious history takes the historical timeframe beyond the ancient Near East into the continuum of the two major world religions, of Judaism and Christianity.[3]

The ultimate format of the Hebrew Bible is that imparted to it by the process of development outlined above. It is, in fact, a resource or library for the religion associated with one particular deity — Yahweh. That deity is in turn associated with one particular society, called, by the collection, Israel. The contents of the Hebrew Bible have been drawn together by various stages of literary composition and editing to enlighten the reader about the manner in which the God of Israel has operated in the past history of the people and so to give roots to a contemporary understanding of the Yahwistic religion. Ultimately all the material contained in the Hebrew Bible is taken as applying to one God. This deity has a personal name, YHWH, which God himself reveals in Exodus 3. This God is presented as an adult male figure, but one lacking divine parents, siblings or children. The surface level of the Hebrew text reveals a solitary figure, lacking even a partner or consort. This leaves a vacuum, a lack of family which is balanced by human beings who can be described as 'sons of God'. Hence the intimate connection between the idea of God and that of Israel in this Yahwistic library.

Yet beneath the apparent monotheism of the works there is a great deal of diversity in religious thought present in the collection. To take one example, in Genesis 1 – 11 the same deity is presented both as benevolent creator and blesser of human beings and as a person who chooses to annihilate all that has been created by him. Can the same person act in totally opposing ways to the same group of people and remain a whole character? Or, taking the theme of a divine leader of armies in Deuteronomy, does this image cohere with that of a woman labouring to give birth, in Isaiah?

This book seeks to investigate the many images of God and the conflicting impressions of God as a person to be found in the Old Testament. In this introduction I have used two differing definitions of the material to be examined — the Hebrew Bible and the Old Testament. It is necessary to explain the relationship between these terminologies. By Hebrew Bible is meant the texts written mostly in Hebrew which form the so-called Masoretic text of Jewish Scripture; this is organized in three parts, Law, Prophets and Writings (see Table on p. 4). By Old Testament is meant the version of this material to be found in Christian Bibles, including some texts not in Hebrew Scripture, being written in Greek, but coming from a background in early Judaism.[4] The present book will take the three-part format of the Hebrew texts but will draw on works which are derived from the wider source such as the Wisdom of Solomon. The intention, then, is to explore a variety of images of the Old Testament God, taken from particular texts within the Yahwistic collection. In order to establish a foundation for further study the first exploration will consist of a discussion of Genesis 1 – 11, chapters which function as an introduction to the topic of God and introduce some basic divine characteristics.

The chapters on law (Torah) develop three separate images of God. On the surface God is a single figure; the text of Torah links the creator deity with the one who founds a nation by selecting one clan and making personal commitments with its leader in successive generations. Thus the command of God in Genesis 1 to multiply and fill the earth is fulfilled in a special way with the expansion of a clan to twelve tribes and hence to a whole nation. The deity who oversees this process is at the same time Lord God, God Almighty, God of the Fathers, revealed in Exodus 3 as owning a personal name now revealed for the first time to a chosen human being. But within the narrative are traces of another reality. The names and functions of other gods exist within the present text of Torah. Something of the past polytheistic history of God in Israelite society can be uncovered here.

But what about the role of any, or all, ancient divine beings? Does the existence of the world at large and its dynamisms owe anything to divine activity? Is it possible that there is a single planned purpose to the universe? The world often appears to be a chaotic place, and it seems that human behaviour can be likewise random activity in response to individual situations. In contrast to this picture the concept of law, covenant and order offers a major image of God in Torah. A single deity as source of world order opens the way to an image of a single character: Deuteronomy posits that the face of this God is one of love and jealousy, a mixture of two extremes of nurturing patient care and determined and crushing violence.

Chart of Old Testament texts in canonical collections

39 books in Hebrew and Protestant Christian Bibles
46 in Catholic Christian Bibles

Torah / Pentateuch

Genesis
Exodus
Leviticus
Numbers
Deuteronomy

Prophets
Former (also called Deuteronomistic Histories)

Joshua
Judges
1, 2 Samuel (in Greek Bible = 1, 2 Kings)
1, 2 Kings (in Greek Bible = 3, 4 Kings)

Latter

(Major)	(The twelve minor)			
Isaiah	Hosea	Obadiah	Nahum	Haggai
Jeremiah	Joel	Jonah	Habakkuk	Zechariah
Ezekiel	Amos	Micah	Zephaniah	Malachi

Writings

Psalms	Lamentations
Job	Esther
Proverbs	Daniel
Ecclesiastes / Qohelet	Ezra
Ruth	Nehemiah
Song of Songs	1, 2 Chronicles (in Greek Bible = Paralipomenon)

Deutero-canonical texts found in Catholic Christian Bibles

Judith
Tobit
Baruch
1, 2 Maccabees
Ecclesiasticus (Sirach)
Wisdom of Solomon

These are found in the Greek Bible but not in the Hebrew collection.

The prophetic literature reveals the development of this concept of God as a single deity in Israelite–Jewish religion.[5] Such a god can both make personal contracts with others and demand that they fulfil their reciprocal obligations. Despite the majestic tone of many passages, however, prophecy continues to align this universal god with human language, so, for instance, the deity can be addressed by human beings as husband and as father. In turn the deity speaks through prophetic intermediaries of humans as partners defaulting on marriage agreements or ignoring the proper social role of daughters. Even the focus on masculine social roles is broadened here, to image God as pregnant woman and nursing mother.

The single nature of God is stretched by this application of competing metaphors. But one type of imagery which underlies several OT texts, so creating some common ground, is that of mythology. Ezekiel opens with the image of a throne-chariot god, an image itself derived from cultic language and reflecting a mythological world-view which gives a foundation for temple worship. In this cultic framework Jerusalem functions as Mount Zion and so is the counterpart of God's heavenly home. This image brings the reader of the Bible into a world of ideas and pictures unfamiliar to the twentieth-century Westerner but evidenced from the work of archaeologists of Near Eastern history — a world of winged cherubs and wheeled thrones, of blazing fire and watery chaos.[6]

The Writings are, by definition, less of a coherent collection than either Law or Prophecy. They contain several self-contained categories of literature such as Wisdom books and Psalms. In these texts a further selection of divine images can be found. God can be described through his attributes which have a semi-separate identity. God's wisdom, his powers of thought and reason, become the Wisdom of God, a force which can leave the transcendent sphere and be located in the human world, in people, in teachings, in texts. Yet, ultimately, this wisdom returns to God, just as God's spirit also returns from the human form to the deity who breathed it out.[7] All paths turn back to the God at the centre of the universe and to metaphors which endorse the divine centrality.

Among these one of the most popular concepts is that of God as king, source of all power and authority, the supermodel of leadership as humanly conceived. The kingship of the God of Israel establishes and maintains world order. Seated on his throne, God rules over all aspects of human existence, from social order to the fertility of the land.

Such a deity may, on the surface, have little to do with a scientific modern language of social definition. A frequent modern concern is about 'rights' — human, civil, animal. Could the Old Testament offer relevant information for this topic? It is precisely God the universal king who is connected with the terms 'justice' and 'righteousness'. These are powers of God, his throne companions, that is, spiritual beings which surround and guard the divine judgement seat. These transcendent powers reach out through God's commanding speech to establish order in the universe, in wind and rain, and in human society. Prosperity and adversity for human beings are the consequence of God's judicial activity. But is there a visible divine response to order and disorder in human affairs? Job and Ecclesiastes challenge the reader to view God as weak and oppressive and yet still appropriate this deity as the basic foundation for human understanding of the origins and goal of the universe.

Finally, the book of Daniel is unsure of its position in the OT collection, being placed in the Writings in the Hebrew Bible and in Prophecy in the Greek Septuagint version of the OT. Modern scholarship labels it Apocalypse because of its subject-matter, thus making it a work on its own in the OT. There are many existing texts of ancient Jewish or Christian apocalypses but these are outside Scripture. Daniel thus offers a bridge between the traditions of the OT and the wider variety of surviving texts from Judaism of the Second Temple period. The perspective of the book is that of time and history. Is there a purpose attached to the succession of world empires in the ancient Near East; what could that underlying purpose be and how might it affect Jews faithful to their ancestral Yahwistic traditions?

At this point a modern reader may echo the ancient text by asking 'What has God to do with us?' It is a valid question in biblical terms since the whole variety of God in the Old Testament has to do with human understanding. God is continually dealt with in relation to human existence. Whether as one who breaks into human reality as a stranger on the road (Genesis 18) or as fire and storm (Exodus 19), or as one perceived as a principle of order 'under the sun' (Ecclesiastes), God is everywhere a character engaged in relationship with his creation. Genesis 1 suggests that humans are made in the image of God. To see a human being is then to see God. But what exactly is the content of this mirroring of God and humanity? There are issues to develop here, of what constitutes the essence of divinity and of humanity. Is imaging God's perfection the aim of human life, for instance?[8] Or is the challenge to view the scope of divine power through the prism of human fragmented behaviour — sometimes peaceful, sometimes violent?

Focusing on person and individual is paired with an approach to group, society and world environment. A twentieth-century reader may well talk of being a world citizen by birth and becoming a religious person by adult choice. These two forms of group membership, of society and religious community, have then to be balanced against each other. But in the biblical world there is no such reality as secular society.

All human activity is also the scene of divine action, right down to conception and birth.[9] God cannot be neglected in political, economic or social affairs. But how does the modern reader feel about the biblical presentation of God? Are we happy with a general, a veteran of war, ready to swing into action with thunderbolt and wipe out the earth's inhabitants? Or the predominantly masculine figure who views the female as a subordinate being whose image is suitable to express negative values and to take responsibility for the severance of relationships between God and his people?

Exploring biblical images of God raises for the reader issues of contemporary relevance. It is possible for a given reader to select within the diversity of language those images which, for him or her, offer a means of communication with the sphere of transcendent order. This raises matters to do with readers' expectations of text and of the role of biblical language. In the area of readerly reactions it is possible for a person to 're-use' the diverse images found in the original texts and also to plug into the unity implied in the term 'God' since each chosen textual resource indeed offers 'God' to the reader, whether this be one particular image of the deity or a given theme such as time or male or female imagery.

Notes

1   Cf. here J. Miles, *God: A Biography* (New York: Simon & Schuster, 1995).

2   Cf. here modern scholarly interpretations of the connection between Israelite history and literature. For a challenging account see P. R. Davies, *In Search of Ancient Israel* (Sheffield: Sheffield Academic Press, 1992).

3   This comment assumes a continuity of interpretation between collections of material taken as 'inspired' text by two major world religions and the previously existing literature. But this does not mean that these collections were exactly the same. The discovery of biblical texts at Qumran in the Judaean desert, dating from the first century CE, which are the same books as found in the OT while having significant differences of wording, indicate the fluidity of text within a particular literary work. Books arose from a process of editing, adding and subtracting phrases, and not from the pen of a single writer. Moreover the OT works found in the Jewish Bible are not the same in detail as similar works in the Christian Bible, nor do all Christian communities have exactly the same number of books in their authorized collections. Yet, in both world religions, there came a time when fluidity ceased and the task became one of copying out an agreed text which, further on, came to be part of an agreed collection of books.

4   'Masoretic' derives from the name of a particular school of early Jewish scholars who studied and copied the Hebrew Bible. They are called by modern scholars the Masoretes and their text of Hebrew Scripture became the text adopted by rabbinic Judaism. The Masoretes put vowel signs into the Hebrew texts which

gave only the consonants of which a word was composed. The reader was presumed to know enough Hebrew to read the word allowing for vowel sounds separating each consonant; however the decline of Hebrew as a spoken language resulted in the need to indicate to a reader how each word must be pronounced. Concerning the fluidity of text tradition, see also note 3 above. A discussion about the diversity attached to text development is to be found in P. R. Davies, *Whose Bible Is It Anyway?* (Sheffield: Sheffield Academic Press, 1995).

5   Isaiah 40 onwards uses the term 'God' to describe a universal deity, a concept understood in opposition to the polytheistic context of older religion, for example. In this setting a cosmic trial takes place which offers judgement on the gods of the surrounding nations.

6   The best method of accessing this type of information is to consult J. B. Pritchard (ed.), *Ancient Near Eastern Texts Relating to the Old Testament* (Princeton: Princeton University Press, 1969) — especially the volume of illustrations.

7   As with wisdom so with spirit. God's spirit (*ruach*) is a force which is breathed into human beings in Genesis 2 to give them life.

8   'Perfection' here means completion, fulfilment of existence. God could be said to have complete knowledge and so complete wisdom. God can foresee accurately the consequence of all his actions and so can make the right moves to achieve his plans. Another approach would be to say that God 'loves' himself and his creation since he can carry through his own identity into purposeful action and enjoy the results. However, God does sometimes have to learn to adapt to failure: as in the Flood story in Genesis.

9   In the stories of the Patriarchs God controls the life of a family, especially the important aspect of children to carry on the family name. The entire plot tension in the Abraham stories is built around this theme, with God, Abraham, Sarah and Hagar all competing to control the process of producing an heir for Abraham.

2 Introducing God, Genesis 1 – 11

The first part of this introduction outlined a task to be pursued, a search for the images of God in the Old Testament. The next stage is to begin that search. But how or where to begin? It has already been stated that there are many diverse ideas of divine identity in the OT. How can any one image be given priority? There is a strong possibility of total fragmentation here. Since it is necessary to start from somewhere, however, it is not a bad idea to start where the present OT begins, with the ideas about God revealed by the first eleven chapters of Genesis. The final editor of the OT collection has allowed these chapters concerning the creation of the world and of human existence to lead the way into the story of Israel; by doing so this editor has given priority to certain facets of the deity and made them into key images which will be replayed in other works within the collection.

Although these first chapters have a chronological dimension — they start 'In the beginning' (Gen 1:1) and move on through the 'generations of the heavens and the earth' (Gen 2:4) to the generations of human beings — their significance is not that of documentary history but rather they are stories with a timeless meaning. They record events outside history, since they all occur before history, that is, the history of Israel, which properly begins with the story of Abraham. In order to understand their significance the reader has to accept a particular interpretation of the term 'history'; this is not to be taken in the modern idiom as a scientific record of exactly how past events took place, but rather as a metaphor for the tradition concerning past generations. In this way Israelite history begins with the name of the first major ancestor of the nation. The earlier stories of the origins of the world at large and of human society function as a prelude to history and stand outside its framework but still offering a commentary on historical events.

Scholars call this type of narrative 'myth'.[1] This can be misleading since the modern reader takes the word 'mythical' to mean of little value. But these myths are of great value since they answer the eternal questions humans ask, such as:

- Where do I / we come from?
- Who am I / are we?
- Why are we here?
- What are the boundaries of our existence?

The first chapters of the OT, then, are an ancient equivalent of modern scientific explanations of the universe. Members of modern industrial society situate themselves via physics, chemistry and biology. The ancient world situated itself via religious texts explaining the relationship between human experience and the world of supernatural beings whose energies directed the cosmos.

Genesis 1 – 11 produces its explanations in the guise of stories:

Chapters 1 – 2 tell the story of the origins of the universe
Chapters 3 – 5, 11 tell the story of the causes of disruption
Chapters 6 – 9 tell the story of the consequences of disorder

These narratives are to be read not only at their face value but also as providing material for philosophical reflection. In the first chapter of Genesis, for instance, the message is that the universe is an orderly place within which each element has its part to play. This order is the product of a divine plan which itself comes from a rational divine being whose commanding word achieves the goal of beauty in order and separation. The order achieved by God could be labelled 'moral' since it is a reflection of eternal divine truth and stability. Human existence emerges within that framework of morality and is shaped by it.

Although the story of Adam and Eve and Cain and Abel appears to play on a personal individual morality, the focus of the chapters is less on one person's ethical stance and more on the totality of human behaviour. Human beings choose disruption while wishing to better their standing in the world. This leads to disruption at the cosmic level.

The text adopts as ground-plan the idea that God, the world and human beings are forces tied into a single set of relationships. Good relations between humans and the deity mean that the earth achieves its perfect state of cultivation in Genesis 2 with the arrival of Adam (dust creature) from the *adamah* (dust), whereas a disruption of divine–human relations in Genesis 3 leads to a consequent fragmentation of the relationship between humans and their physical environment. The full extent of the disruption of good order and its results are pictured in the Flood stories. The opening of a gap in relations between God and human society develops into a total divine rejection of humankind and of the earth which has sustained them.

There is here a play on the theme of order and disorder, of creation and of chaos. In the beginning the world was a watery chaos which God made fruitful by order and separation of the waters to allow earth and heavens to appear, thus providing space for plant and animal life. In the Flood God allows chaos to take over again and so to destroy all life. This tension between life and death, between creation and chaos, situates the character of the deity in these chapters. It makes of God the pivotal figure, the true and single arbiter of the destiny of the universe. God here is the principle of world order, a being who enjoys viewing what his mental blueprint looks like when transposed to the material world and yet who is also a solitary voice roaring across the waters.[2]

Within this context three particular images of God take shape:

- God the creator
- God the judge
- God the redeemer

Both by speech and by shaping the material world God acts as creator in Genesis 1 − 2. As creator God is a responsible figure; God takes care of his creation and in particular seeks intimacy with humankind. There is on God's part a benevolent interest in what he has formed which provides a strong contrast with the divine attitude which emerges in Genesis 3. There a kindly being seeks to meet with human friends then changes suddenly into a person who stands aside from erstwhile companions, sharply condemning their actions and rejecting any parity between them. In the full flowering of this identity as judge God presides over the deliberate destruction of all living beings, a judgement which for most of the creatures involved is without mercy. But one man, Noah, finds favour with God. This leads into the third character of God, that of redeemer. After the waters subside God repents of his attack on humans since they are subordinate creatures without the power to act in perfect order at all times. To Noah (Gen 9) God promises an eternal contract of alliance between the deity and his creation, swearing never to destroy the world again.

Within the context of the OT God has become part of a chronological process. As the development of human beings is related as an unfolding narrative, so too God's character is progressively developed. It is possible to approach God here using modern literary criticism. In this manner the OT can be regarded as a form of biography and can be studied as such. Recently J. Miles[3] has produced a study of this kind in which he traces the development of God's identity across the Hebrew Scriptures. Such a process involves reading the text at surface level and taking it as a literary unity.

Following this approach, Miles details the changes in God. In the beginning God is alone and has no experience of relationship. By creating a world of beings God gives himself the opportunity to experience the nature of relationship. In the earliest stages this experience is beneficent. God offers and receives a loving regard. But then God discovers that relationship can be unstable; his temperament takes a violent turn and he condemns that which he himself brought into being. God is a disturbing character 'as anyone is disturbing who holds immense power and seems not to know what he wants to do with it ...'[4] In the scenes which follow Adam and Eve's departure from the garden God is alternately tender and hostile, creator and destroyer. A basic shape for God's character in the OT is established here; one which Miles describes as flawed by a fissure between these two contradictory divine roles.[5]

This is one style of reading the OT. Another, and one adopted by modern biblical research, is to take the text apart in an attempt to discover the smaller individual units which have been combined by ancient editors to produce the present text. This approach would separate the two stories of creation, for instance, in Genesis 1 and 2 since the deity in the first is El (God) and in the second is YHWH-El (Lord God). It is possible to arrive, then, at a number of different but parallel images of God within a given text. Using this as a base one can read, in these chapters, not a chronological development of the potentialities of God's character, but several images of God which can be put alongside one another simultaneously.

In this context, too, God appears to be a complex being in which the roles of creator, judge and redeemer are interwoven. The final story of the early chapters of Genesis, the Tower of Babel account (Gen 11), provides a sophisticated image here. The people of the world want to stay together and so they build a great tower as a focal point for human society. It could well be argued that this is indeed a way of fulfilling God's original blessing of humankind which implied peace and good relations between them.

But God is unhappy. He distrusts their power and decides to destroy their plans by diversifying their language. Is God not defeating his own purpose here? Is he not, in fact, suffering from jealousy in seeing human organization as a challenge to his power? So God judges and condemns, but by destroying social unity he causes humans to separate from one another and migrate across the face of the earth. Thus, in the end, God's original blessing is fulfilled, that human beings should multiply and fill the earth. Thus is redemption brought out of judgement.

The interweaving of the three images of God as creator, judge and redeemer not only provides evidence for images of God, it also offers a means of commenting on human history. The images of creator, judge and redeemer frequently offer biblical writers the means of defining human experience in a divine context. In the prophetic books, for example, God is spoken of as the one who founded Israel, its creator, but as one who now condemns it and will bring it down. The image of judge here allows readers a new light on political events such as invasion by a foreign power. Yet the prophets speak finally of a hope beyond chaos and destruction of the state, of a new Israel, of a remnant who will return and rebuild Judah. Isaiah describes the God who will bring this about as Israel's redeemer (cf. Isa 44:6). New political developments including the repopulation and redevelopment of land acquire added significance through this religious commentary.

The many voices of the Psalms, in the Writings section of the Hebrew Scriptures, bless God for his original creation of the world and look for future renewal. Thus Psalm 104 tells of God's creative work in detail and goes on to reflect on God's breath of life which brings all life into being. When God takes his breath away death ensues, but when he breathes out again his spirit renews the face of the earth (verses 27–30). Thus is the whole cycle of human life brought within the context of the divine life energy.

The book of Job offers another variation on these themes. The book opens with a creator in charge of the universe. In the discourses between Job and his friends God becomes a stern judge whose justice is in dispute. The creator God reappears in the whirlwind scene where God speaks from the heart of the storm about his role as unique creator of the cosmos (Job 38 – 41). Finally God redeems the fortunes of Job in the closing section of the book and vindicates Job's anger at an apparently silent and impassive world order.

Thus Genesis 1 – 11 offer the reader not only an opening to the idea of God in these chapters but also a tool-kit for understanding the deity across the several different texts and literary styles of the Hebrew Bible. This interaction between its different sections reflects the world-view of the final editorial layer of the collection. The last people to put the text in order were monotheists. They believed that the God YHWH was exclusively the universal power who ordered all events. This deity was only partly to be considered in human terms. Thus although God had speech and reason, vision and arm, he was disembodied voice and the space he occupied was that of the universe itself, clouds as clothes and light as ornament.[6]

Such a deity is powerful because he is a single figure and is to be regarded as a reliable source of power and authority. If he has order as a major principle of action then this sets the necessary tone for human society. Human order reflects divine order when human society abides by a code of law. In Torah the consequence of this attitude is that the pivot on which Law turns is the meeting with God at Sinai where God himself tells Israel what their human code of conduct must be.

At the same time a single deity must sometimes be a lonely figure. In his relations with Israel God chooses humans as members of a divine family, his sons. In other ancient religions humans are slaves of the gods, mere robotic servants with no individual identity. By contrast, in Torah God calls Abraham by name (Gen 17), while the prophet Isaiah claims that God is never ignorant of his servant Jacob / Israel and his / their fate (Isa 40:27).

Reading God in this manner as a single, developing character provides one approach to the text of the OT, one suggested to the mind of the reader by the monotheism of the final text. In tension with this approach is that of scholars who operate from the fragmented and diverse images of the deity suggested by the underlying diversity of the text. In this second line of thought each book must be treated individually in terms of its meaning and, indeed, parts of a single book must also be studied in this way.

In the chapters which follow it is the second of these two approaches which takes precedence. Some of the possibilities offered by the monotheism of the OT have been reviewed. From that foundation it will now be possible to investigate the diversity of images of the deity carried by texts. In this approach one can talk not of 'God' but of many 'gods', since each image of the divine is to be taken seriously in its own right as the image of God belonging to a unique piece of text.

Notes

1   Some ancient cultures have left traces of entire cycles of myths (stories about the gods which explain the nature of the deities and their interaction with human beings), thus, for instance, the gods of Greece and Rome. The OT does not contain a comprehensive cycle of myth, although Genesis 1 – 11 is mythological writing whose message is not about one human couple or a deity in action in just one time period. For a commentary on the universalism of these chapters see C. Westermann, *Genesis: A Practical Commentary* (Grand Rapids: Eerdmans, 1987). For more information on types of writing in the OT see G. W. Coats (ed.), *Saga, Legend, Tale, Novella, Fable* (Sheffield: Sheffield Academic Press, 1980) and B. Otzen, H. Gottlieb and K. Jeppesen, *Myths in the Old Testament* (London: SCM Press, 1980).

2   This comment depends to some extent on the interpretation of the phrase 'voice of God'. God in the OT is often represented by voice — the sound of thunder and wind accompanying a great storm — and metaphorically God can roar from his heavenly home. Storm theophany thus provides a major religious image of the deity. See here J. J. Niehaus, *God at Sinai* (Carlisle: Paternoster, 1995), pp. 23, 27–8.

3   See note 1 above.

4   J. Miles, *God: A Biography* (New York: Simon & Schuster, 1995), p. 35.

5   Miles (1995), p. 46.

6   God as a body which can wear clothes is part of OT imagery, although the divine body is not completely anthropomorphized. God's home and clothing are cosmic items which function as garments and rich ornament function for earthly rulers. For texts which reflect these images see, for instance, Psalm 50(49), Psalm 77(76), Isaiah 40:20–23, Ezekiel 1:26–28. See also M. Z. Brettler, *God Is King: Understanding an Israelite Metaphor* (Sheffield: Sheffield Academic Press, 1989) who deals with the parallel between the splendour of kings and God's splendour in the OT.

Section A
Torah

3 *God and gods in Genesis*

The previous chapter established a basis for the exploration of God in the Old Testament. It was suggested there that the present form of the OT allows the first eleven chapters of Genesis to stand by themselves as setting the terms under which God's activities will be described later in the collection. Clearly, one of the major facets of the presentation of God in Genesis 1 – 11 is an overall sense of consistency. One deity dominates the text and is the source of events, from the original creation of an ordered cosmos to the re-establishment of an inhabited world in chapters 10 – 11. The foil to God here is human action: references to any other gods in heaven are, in effect, non-existent.

This single deity is referred to in Genesis 1 – 11 both by the general term for God — El / Elohim — and by a specific marker YHWH or YHWH-El.[1] The character of this deity is complex: at first a beneficent creator but then a powerful destroyer. Responsibility for this character shift is laid not on the unpredictability of the deity but on the corruption of human behaviour. In this way God is allowed to emerge as a reasonably consistent figure while still retaining contradictory impulses.

Chapter 12 of Genesis moves on to a new stage in the theological history of Israel recounted in the OT. The appearance of Abraham (Abram) in chapter 11 opens the door to the founding of one particular people, among the many nations of the world. Genesis 12 is, in this sense, a new beginning. But it would be easy for a reader to slide over the significance of this chapter, lulled by the continuity created through the control which the character of the deity has over the plot of Genesis.

In Genesis 12 the same God acts again, not relating to the human species in general[2] nor to Noah[3] but to another individual human being. The calling of Abram (later called Abraham) to commitment to God's purpose and his apparent willingness to respond[4] brings the reader of the book across a major seam in the text. Here begins the theme of

God's promises which will recur many times in the rest of the OT. The land issue will be the focus of the Deuteronomist and the Deuteronomistic history books[5] and the theme of Israel as God's sons likewise shapes Torah and prophecy, tying in with a particular promise of relationship between king and God in 2 Samuel 7.[6]

When God appears to Abraham in Genesis 12 and speaks to him of commitment to the divine wishes, this is the first move of a narrative plot which carries the reader forward. While requiring Abraham to migrate God also promises him a son; a promise which looks to its future fulfilment. In narrative literature this entails further scenes of interaction between human being and deity. The reader seeks to know what will happen and so is engaged in the process of 'reading on'.

In this literary framework God can only be further defined and described in relation to Abraham. God is, thus, 'the God of Abraham', that is, the deity who speaks to Abraham and whom Abraham is prepared to worship. The deity whose home is heaven is found, in the text, to travel with the family of Abraham and to be accessible in various geographical locations.[7] There is no other practical method of locating God here. The deity is not fixed as the God of a particular city or of a particular region. Abraham is in direct relationship with this God who is unmediated by fixed cult centres or official rites and an official priesthood. The narrator of the story leaves the reader with two protagonists, Abraham and God.

Even when Abraham travels to foreign parts and, in entering a foreign land, comes under the aegis of the deities who own that land and whose cult is established by the local ruler, as with Pharaoh in Egypt, Abraham's God is in control of events. Pharaoh's marriage to Sarai does not comply with divine plans so God sets it aside. God is indeed a universal figure here. This leads the reader to connect the God of Abraham with the deity who brought all life into being in the earlier chapters of Genesis.

The connection is further developed by the overall narrative techniques of the book. On the one hand there is absolute continuity between the human generations — Abraham begets Isaac who begets Jacob who has twelve sons and thus Israel is founded through one family. The tensions in the narrative concerning human fertility (Abraham, Sarah, Hagar), about the right choice of a wife (Rebekah), about relationships within a complex extended family (for instance Jacob, Leah and Rachel), are held together by the ultimate continuity of one particular genealogical line. The reader is not encouraged to ponder on the injustice to Hagar or to Esau or to speculate on how family development could have been, but rather is focused on the essential continuity between Abraham, Isaac and Jacob.

On the other hand, and paralleling the human scene, is the continuity of divine nature — one deity, *the* God of ..., appears consistently in each human age. This God defines himself within the text by virtue of his relationships to human beings. In Genesis 28:13 for instance, God says to Jacob 'I am the Lord, the God of Abraham your father and the God of Isaac ...'. There is, then, a consistency within the text. God is one deity, a benefactor to a chosen household and its descendants whose activities foster that household's life expectancy. This process climaxes in Exodus 3:6 where the God of the burning bush in Midian declares himself to Moses as 'the God of your father, the God of Abraham, the God of Isaac, and the God of Jacob'. This speech implies that the same deity spoke to Abraham and to each generation until he speaks to Moses in his time also. The tradition is established, now a new note creeps in. For God will give his personal name to Israel through Moses, so that an even closer link can be forged between deity and people.

Modern biblical scholarship has easily recognized this continuity and consistency and has offered commentaries explaining its meaning and value. J. Wellhausen, for instance,[8] thought that the continuity of the character of God was caused by the fact that the entire Pentateuch was written, as it now stands, by editors working in the monarchical and post-monarchical period. In editing earlier material into a coherent text the editors inevitably shaped the manner of God's presentation within the text. Later scholars have investigated the variety of themes and motifs which make up the final text of Genesis.

Thus, C. Westermann[9] has examined the particular role of the Promise Narratives within the story of Abraham. In the overall structure of the Abraham saga the promise of a son is a necessary element linked to the structuring of story through the succession of generations. This promise is accompanied by a second motif, that of promise of land. Both motifs are at work in the middle of the Abraham story, in chapter 15, where verses 1–6 refer to heirs and verses 7–21 to land. Verse 7 links both themes by the reference to the Lord, the deity who is also the source of son / promise hopes, as the god who will bring about the settlement of land. Further detailed subsections can be traced within the son / promise subsections. Abraham is concerned with one son, his heir; but the theme is widened to descendants and to many nations in Genesis 22:15–19. Westermann argues that the original line of the text would be one son since that is the smallest coherent story unit. The storyline has been expanded by the concerns of a later age to show how their generation also fulfils the divine promise of heirs to Abraham.

Abraham as a single character has been spotlighted by J. Van Seters.[10] Genesis gives enough information about Abraham for the reader to construct a rounded personality, with a complex set of responses. But is this figure a true representation, in a modern historical sense, of a man who lived many centuries ago? Van Seters has shown that the Abraham material cannot be taken simply as a record of the second millennium BCE. He points to many inconsistencies of the historical framework of the Abraham material. Knowledge drawn from archaeological research and brought to bear on these narratives shows incongruities of detail. He argues, for instance, that the archaic designations for indigenous populations in the stories are not used in the manner of the historical and archaeological realities of the second millennium BCE but are closer to being the idealized image of a much later age.

The attempt to explain the Abraham narratives as historically accurate through comparison with archaeological findings has been pursued by other scholars also.[11] In these comparative studies points of contact between Abraham's life and records of customs of other ancient Near Eastern cultures of the second millennium have been highlighted. One example of this is the suggestion that Abraham's pretence that Sarah is his sister is not mere literary invention by the author; Hurrian marriage customs appear to speak of brother–sister marriage. Scholars are, then, divided between those who side with Van Seter's approach and those who would consider that the text has a serious foundation in ancient history.

A. Alt opened up yet another dimension on this issue with his pursuit of the God of the Fathers.[12] He worked from the basis that the text of Genesis as it now stands is an editorial work of a later period, but he argued that earlier layers of religious tradition can still be found within the final text. Alt took as evidence for this the titles of God in these patriarchal stories and suggested the existence within the text of a composite deity who has absorbed the separate names and titles of three separate clan deities:

- the God of Abraham
- the Fear of Isaac
- the Bull / Champion of Jacob

Each of these gods, Alt suggests, was the particular god of one family unit and was associated with the territorial space of that clan. Jacob's god, for instance, appears in the book as a deity connected with the use of Beersheba as a sacred place where sacrifice can be offered. Statements such as that of Jacob in Genesis 31:5, 'the God of my father has been with me', imply a particular deity who can be defined not by a place or region but with reference to one human being.

Alt's thesis, based on these arguments, is that each separate clan originally had its own deity, but as groups merged into a broader tribal society each deity was accommodated within a common theme — the God of the fathers. This accommodation paved the way for the development of a more rigidly monotheistic treatment of the identity of the God of Israel.

References to earlier levels of religious belief within the OT have been put into new perspective by the progress of archaeological research since the 1940s. It has become clear that there was an overall pattern of polytheism in the North West Semitic region and that this is connected with worship of a pantheon whose high god was El. Thus, for instance, the discovery of Ras Shamra (ancient Ugarit) and the exploration of it as the site of an ancient city has brought to bear a broader field of religious experience as the context for Genesis. M. H. Pope's work in the 1950s on the Ugaritic pantheon[13] and on the figure of the high god of the city set Genesis in a polytheistic frame. It was now clear that the word 'El' is not only a generic term for 'God' but also a personal name of a particular deity, one well known in the West Semitic region of the ancient Near East. This deity, frequently represented as an ancient figure seated on a throne, was the high god, convenor of the council of the gods and source of decisions on world affairs. This is 'Father El' or even 'Grandfather El'. Pope's work formed the basis for that of later scholars such as F. M. Cross who argued a direct link between Canaanite religion and the religion of Israel.[14]

This line of thought is not only useful for the OT background in general. It has specific import for the study of Genesis, which frequently employs the word 'El / Elohim'. In the final version of the text Elohim is a word for God whose actual name is YHWH. But it is possible to see here the interweaving of different levels of tradition. It is odd that a single deity should be known by a plural 'gods' (elohim). This may well be the effect of bringing an older polytheistic approach to religion into line with a later monotheistic one. It would be possible to read the first chapter of Genesis as an account of how the gods created the world and made human beings in their own image (Gen 1:26). As we have noted, chapter 2 of the book has a particular name for the deity, that of YHWH-El (Lord God). Here it seems the two deities have been brought together as though they were one figure. Later on in the text,[15] titles are applied to the Lord as due to him. However these phrases translated as 'Almighty God' and 'Everlasting God' were essentially titles of majesty describing El — so, 'The Mighty El' and 'El, the Everlasting One'. The story of the golden calf in Exodus may be a trace of some distinction which came to be made between the 'Bull El' and the Lord of Israel.

Genesis then, is not a text of such apparent simplicity or unity as may at first appear. Explorations of Canaanite deities made by scholars such as L. K. Handy[16] have argued that polytheism should be regarded as the original religion of the West Semitic region, one shared by the historical ancient Israelites as part of the local culture. In a recent article[17] Handy states that:

it is impossible to dismiss the picture of a religious world based on a pantheon ... sufficient artifactual material has been excavated from the regions of the two petty states of Israel and Judah to support the notion that the populace revered more than just the single deity.[18]

He argues for the existence, in historical Israel, of a four-tiered pantheon not unlike that which is evidenced at ancient Ugarit. At the top were the royal couple. After them came the major active deities, followed by the craft deities, specialists whose expertise was used by the major deities. At the bottom of this hierarchy were the slaves of the divine realm, the messengers. In the OT texts the royal couple would be YHWH / El and Asherah (evidence for Asherah can be found in Chapter 9 below, on God and wisdom). The bottom rank of messengers is paralleled in the OT by the angels. As for the second rank of gods, prophetic attacks on other gods include a knowledge of Baal, Shemesh, Yareah, Mot:

The prophetic admonitions against priests, prophets and rulers ... demonstrate that these deities were established in the official religion as it was practised at the time.[19]

One major recent work on this topic of the religion of ancient Israel has been that of M. Smith.[20] Smith points out in his introduction that he is extending the work of earlier scholars who had highlighted the El references in the OT. Smith aims to expand earlier work to produce a history of the deity in Israel.

Starting with the religious situation of the biblical time of the judges, Smith uses archaeological evidence to show that polytheism was the culture of the region. Israel's God can, without difficulty, be fitted into that basis, since the OT evidences a running together of El and YHWH:

Like some descriptions of Yahweh, some of Yahweh's epithets can be traced to those of El. Traditions concerning the cultic site of Shechem illustrate the cultural process lying behind the Yahwistic ... assimilation to old cultic sites of El.[21]

The biblical texts tell of a deviance among the people; how they went off to worship Baal and the Asherahs. But these names are also familiar from Ugaritic texts. In the poems of Baal and Anat, Baal is a vigorous son of El who demands his own home and fights against his siblings Death (Mot) and Sea (Yam). Baal is the god of storm and thus of fertility. This image of God is not unfamiliar to readers of the OT where it is always attached to the Lord of Israel. In the same way Israel's deity is not unlike the goddess Anat for she is a deity of war and battle and bloody victory:

Although Anat was not a goddess in Israel, her savage battling in the Ugaritic Baal cycle ... has been often compared with numerous biblical passages.[22]

The OT texts speak of the Asherahs as, on the one hand, trees and pillars, that is, cultic objects and, on the other, of Asherah as a female deity, Queen of Heaven. In Ugarit she is the wife of El and mother of gods, a figure to be solemnly reverenced.

Although the OT implies the existence of these deities as sources of deceit for the Israelites, this is probably not to be taken as the whole story. Smith's chapter on Yahweh and Baal suggests that originally the dwellers in the Canaanite highlands shared in El–Asherah worship. At a time when El was falling out of favour as the main image of supernatural power and his role was taken by the younger gods, Ugarit and other cities put their trust in Baal, but the Israelite group took up the deity YHWH instead. As the highlands of Canaan became a political force, so the deity of that area took precedence over the other deities. At the time of the kings of Judah and Israel only one national deity really mattered. This god was the one who spoke up for the nation in the council of the gods and through whose covenant with the king came order and prosperity for the nation.

Smith suggests in his next chapter that the finding of a religious tablet at Kuntillet Arjud which seemingly shows Yahweh with a consort indicates that the linking of YHWH and El led to Asherah becoming YHWH's partner. There is evidence, too, that Israel connected their Lord with the sun deity. In the religious reforms referred to in 2 Kings, horses and chariot are destroyed; these items probably represented the vehicle in which the sun travels around the sky. Pictures of this theme have been found within Egyptian religion.[23] Smith turns next to Israelite religious practices and suggests that there is some evidence that early Israel knew of child sacrifice (the *MoLeCH* sacrifice) and of worship of the ancestors. All of this makes the older religion of Israel very different from an exclusive monotheism. For Smith the move to monotheism came later in the life of Israel, in the Exile, for instance:

The development towards monotheism in Israel involved complex processes of convergence and differentiation of deities.

The inclusion of solar language for Yahweh, the acceptance of the symbol of the asherah and the cultic sites of the high places, the numerous practices pertaining or relating to the dead, long escaped priestly, Deuteronomistic and prophetic criticism.[24]

Not all scholars are in agreement with this approach to Syro-Palestinian religion. J. De Moor[25] has argued against the view that polytheism dominated the Judaean pantheon for a long period of time and posited the early arrival of monotheism to Israel. Starting with the biblical account, De Moor points out the existence of a number of human names which are made up of a Y-h element in the accounts of Israel before the age of David. This leads him to suggest that the area had already adopted a single deity at this time.

In order to explain how this could be, De Moor goes back in time to the reign of Akhnaten in Egypt.[26] This monarch is known from the Amarna evidence to have become a monotheist and to have offended many of his more important subjects by this move. De Moor links Akhnaten's religious change with a general unrest among the cultures of Egypt, Mesopotamia and Ugarit over the old divine pantheons which they had been worshipping. The political and social upheavals of this Late Bronze Age period led to shifts in religious focus, such as the rise of Baal in Ugaritic tradition evidenced from the clay tablets found in the city ruins.

Connected with the time of Akhnaten, there is Egyptian evidence for an extremely powerful Canaanite official at the Egyptian court, by the name of Beya. De Moor sees in this figure the historical Moses. He points out the unusually great influence which Beya wielded at the height of his power, including the unique privilege of building his own tomb in the Valley of the Kings. This tomb is little adorned with religious symbols or signs of the Egyptian gods:

it is surely remarkable that ... the tomb of Beya remained small and unadorned ... Could it be that Beya did not want to bow to the images of the gods of Egypt because his own religion forbade him to do so?[27]

When the dynasty fell Beya had to flee. Here De Moor turns back to the OT. He regards Balaam's speech in Numbers 23:9 as referring to the hope that Beya / Moses and his small company of warriors brought to Canaan when he returned there. For this was a time of destabilization. The upheavals in Egypt deprived the area of its usual overlord at a time when the Sea Peoples were pushing their conquests into the coastal plains. Moses brought hope of a Canaanite revival but without ultimately being able to drive the invaders out of the land. Moses found a haven in Bashan where he was able to build a monotheistic culture based on the religious constitutions set out in the law codes of the Torah. These ancient events were recorded in Psalm 68 and in Deuteronomy 32 − 33. The theme of God's triumphant march from the south should be viewed, for De Moor, as the memory of Moses's march to a safe site for the implanting of his own religion and society. In this tradition theocracy had a central place and later it formed a means of critiquing human kingship patterns.

In this argument De Moor has brought to bear on the OT the evidence not so much of ancient Canaan as of ancient Egypt. By means of this evidence De Moor ultimately tends to support the scholarly view, long held, that the non-monarchical religion was a monotheism older than that of royal polytheistic cults:

Moses ... was the lawgiver who prevented Yahwism from merging completely with Baalism, the competing new religious movement in Canaan at the end of the Late Bronze Age.[28]

It is sometimes possible to trace his influence, an example being the commandment not to make any graven image of God. This fits with Moses / Beya's Egyptian background:

Akhnaten had vetoed all images of deities and the Amun-Re theology had been obliged to counter this radicalism in formulating the doctrine that Amun-Re could not be depicted since no artist knew his real shape.[29]

Also the disappearance of certain styles of figuring goddesses in Early Iron Age sites argues for a monotheistic influence at work:

Thus it would seem possible that Moses who, if he may be identified with Beya, knew from personal experience how difficult it was to draw a clean borderline between simple portrayal and actual worship, added the prohibition to make images to the already existing injunction not to bow to other gods.[30]

De Moor's argument runs counter to M. Smith's view that ancient Israel formed a unity with its surrounding culture and that all Syro-Palestinian religion of these ages was polytheistic at base.

Since, however, the final layer of the OT displays a monotheistic approach the question must be raised as to when this shift occurred. Smith argues that this move was the result of many centuries of gradual change in Judaean religion and that it is to be aligned with the Persian period:

The written works of Ezekiel and second Isaiah permitted a sustained reflection on Israel's history and the nature of the Israelite deity. Out of the process of reflection and writing arose clear expressions of Israelite monotheism.[31]

Smith argues for a reshaping of the reader's understanding of the development of Israelite religion:

the old question of explaining monotheism becomes a new issue of accounting for the phenomenon of convergence, a stage in Israelite religion older than the appearance of monolatry.[32]

There is no way of conclusively verifying which of these two approaches to the ancient religious traditions of Israel is correct. There is simply not enough evidence outside of the OT to prove the exact nature of religion in Israel in the Late Bronze Age and into the Iron Age. The phenomenon of Akhnaten's monotheism is known from archaeological research, but so is the polytheistic nature of religion in the Syro-Palestinian region. Part of the problem here is that scholars do not know enough about the origins of the social unit called Israel. If Israel was continuous in many ways with the social and religious organization of the North West Semitic area, a strong likelihood, then a development from polytheism is supported. However, it is possible that Israel was not only not a city-state on the model of the towns of the coastal plain of Canaan but also that its cultural base was different from the surrounding area, a view consonant with the suggestion that at least some of its founding groups came from outside the immediate locality.

Whichever view a reader adopts it has, however, to take into account the impact of the Ugaritic research undertaken since the 1950s and still continuing. The account of Israelite religion found in the OT has to be examined against the growing record of archaeological information in the twentieth century. Genesis, then, is a text which repays careful study. A first impression of the book is that, despite some peculiarities of expression, there is a single god to be found there. Working against the grain of the overall editing of the material opens up a reader's vision to new vistas of the nature of religious culture which underlies the present text and raises broad but significant issues relating to the overall development of religious thought in ancient Canaan and Israel. This, in turn, challenges the view that major world religions are static and monolithic affairs, the result of a single revelation of deity to human beings. A new pattern, that of the development of religious belief within human societies, opens before the reader's eyes.

Summary

This chapter begins with the overall presentation of God in Genesis 12 – Exodus 3 where a single deity — the god of the fathers — interacts with the founding fathers of Israel. This treatment of text opens out to the traces of polytheism which can be detected under the surface, to comparisons with the high god El and to a consideration of the scope of scholarly debate, taking up the arguments of two contributors to the debate, J. De Moor and M. Smith.

Notes

1 'El' is a Hebrew noun gendered as singular, masculine. It becomes the OT word to describe any deity, i.e. the equivalent of the English word 'God'. But it is now known that it was the proper name of one particular deity in Ugaritic religion. 'Elohim' is the masculine plural of El. As a term for a single deity it is incorrect grammatically, although the OT regularly uses it linked with YHWH. As a general plural it should be translated as 'gods', which could make sense of Genesis 1 where the text would then read, in verse 24 'The gods said "Let us make ..."'. The name YHWH is explained in the OT as the name of Israel's god as revealed by him to Moses. Genesis 2 has the unusual form YHWH-El translated by the RSV as 'Lord God', but with the possible reading of two separate deities now linked together as a composite being.

2 The word 'covenant' does not occur in Genesis 1, but the theme of commitment of deity to humanity is present in the divine blessing of humans in verse 28.

3 God's speech to Noah after the Flood represents a new stage in the development of the term 'covenant'. God's promise of support for future life and fertility is given under the title of an eternal covenant (*berit olam*). See Genesis 9:9.

4 Abraham does migrate and the overall narrative endorses the view that Abraham committed himself to God 'in faith'. However, Abraham is still not totally centred on a belief in the deity since, in chapter 15, he is ready to dismiss God's promises as useless, since he still has no heir.

5 Because of the close similarity of theological message and of vocabulary between Deuteronomy and the histories from Joshua to 2 Kings, scholars believe that one circle produced both of these. Deuteronomy offers a plan for the future which includes blessing and curse, whereas the histories show how that plan worked out in time, with people choosing the way that led to divine curses falling on them. See Chapter 5 of this book for more information on this subject.

6 2 Samuel 7 reflects a new covenant model, from the perspective of the chronology of the OT, but an alternative model if the view is taken that the editing process simply offers readers a choice of parallel attitudes to the meaning of the term 'covenant'. Here it is a royal model as opposed to the Mosaic model offered by the Sinai material.

7 Thus in the Itinerary lists within the Abraham saga, when Abraham reaches his destination he is frequently shown as sacrificing to the deity or meeting with his god there. Cf. here the Oaks of Mamre scenes (Gen 13:18; 18:1). Although the implication of these events is that mountains and groves are holy sites and places of theophany, this is not the same reality as a later level of the OT where there is one central shrine and holy building, i.e. the Temple in Jerusalem.

8 Cf. A. K. Millard and D. J. Wiseman (eds), *Essays on the Patriarchal Narratives* (Leicester: Inter-Varsity Press, 1980), p. 46.

9 C. Westermann, *Genesis: A Practical Commentary* (Grand Rapids: Eerdmans, 1987) and also C. Westermann, *Genesis* (3 vols; Minneapolis: Augsburg Fortress, 1984–86).

10 Cf. J. Van Seters, *Abraham in History and Tradition* (New Haven: Yale University Press, 1975).

11 Cf. M. J. Selman, 'Comparative customs and the Patriarchal Age' in Millard and Wiseman (eds), *Essays on the Patriarchal Narratives*.

12 A. Alt, *Essays on Old Testament History and Religion* (Oxford: Blackwell, 1966).

13 E.g. M. H. Pope, *El in Ugaritic Texts*, Supplement to Vetus Testamentum (1955), and variously in his later works.

14 F. M. Cross, *Canaanite Myth and Hebrew Epic* (Cambridge, MA: Harvard University Press, 1973).

15 These include titles such as 'El Shaddai', 'El Elyon', 'El Olam' and 'El Roi'. All of them have the name El accompanied by a quality defining El, such as the most high / everlasting / whom I have seen.

16 L. K. Handy, *Among the Host of Heaven* (Winona Lake, IN: Eisenbrauns, 1994).

17 L. K. Handy, 'The appearance of pantheon in Judah' in D. Edelman (ed.), *The Triumph of Elohim* (Kampen: Kok Pharos, 1995).

18 Handy (1995), pp. 27–8.

19   Handy (1995), p. 39.
20   M. Smith, *The Early History of God* (New York: Harper & Row, 1990).
21   Smith (1990), p. 11.
22   Cf. Deuteronomy 28 where horrific curses are spoken of by Moses: Smith (1990), p. 61.
23   O. Keel, *The World of Biblical Symbolism* (London: SPCK, 1978).
24   Smith (1990), pp. 161, 163.
25   J. De Moor, *The Rise of Yahwism* (Leuven: Leuven University Press, 1990).
26   Akhnaten is one well-known and frequently referred-to piece of evidence for religion and society in the ancient world. This is because his city, Amarna, was abandoned after the Pharaoh's assassination. It remained fixed at that time level and so provided archaeologists with a good source of material from which to reconstruct this particular era in Egyptian life.
27   De Moor (1990), p. 143.
28   De Moor (1990), p. 169.
29   De Moor (1990), p. 170.
30   De Moor (1990), p. 170.
31   Smith (1990), p. 154.
32   Smith (1990), pp. 155, 156.

4 God of law and covenant in Exodus

The previous chapter focused on the several names and titles for God which have been incorporated into the book of Genesis. Ultimately all references to God(s) have been gathered into a composite picture which has been used to define the God of Israel. This movement comes to a climax in the book of Exodus. In the scene of the burning bush the true name of the Israelite deity is revealed as YHWH. It has to be remembered that, in the ancient world, a name was a vital commodity. The true and personal name of a person incorporated their life force; to know this real name was to have power over the person and to be able to make an intimate relationship with them. When God reveals his name, then, he is inviting Moses and Israel into a personal relationship of trust and loyalty.

The name YHWH is itself important since it conveys the concept of creator and energizer. The exact meaning is debated[1] but whichever form of the verb 'to be' is taken up, the name is connected with life and beingness. God is thus defined as life force, possibly as creator, and as such, a deity who calls Israel into relationship with himself. This same creative being turns into the destroyer in the story of the plagues which follow. In each scene of this story God acts in a harsh manner towards the Egyptians, culminating in his taking of a blood sacrifice from them with the slaying of the firstborn.

The God of Israel here controls the destiny not only of his own people but that of another nation in a foreign land. The gods of the Egyptians cannot resist YHWH's power and might.[2] A figure of cosmic strength emerges in the plague narrative and is endorsed in the scene of the exodus and crossing of the sea. God controls the natural elements, forcing the sea to withdraw and allow God's people through to safety. Exodus 15 sums up the great wonder which this event represents, as do some of the Psalms.[3]

All of this material climaxes in the scenes at Mount Sinai, in the wilderness. The people have left Egypt in order to worship their god in the desert at a holy mountain. The central focus of Exodus is that event, the meeting of God and his servants at Mount Sinai. The narrative stops dead for many chapters while the events at the mountain unfold. Most of this consists of a recital of the law codes which God gave Moses at the mountain meeting, situated in a context of covenant or treaty making. In this manner the spotlight is placed on a god of law and covenant whose image is expanded in the Sinai traditions.

If the question is asked 'Is this large collection of material from the hand of one writer?' the answer is probably 'No'. Modern biblical scholarship has long detected the hand of more than one writer in the text and more than one type of interest in legal matters. It seems that the final form of the material in this part of Torah writings is the result of adding together originally separate elements. The text can be divided as follows:

- Decalogue or Ten Commandments (Exod 20)
- Book of the Covenant (Exod 21 – 23)
- Cultic Code (Lev), including the Holiness Code

Each separate section has its own shape. The Decalogue sets out fundamental principles of religious behaviour, the Book of the Covenant rehearses laws for civil society and the Cultic Code addresses the functions of priests, sacred calendar and patterns of worship. Within this last section the Holiness Code lays out the rules for ritual purity which allow an Israelite to participate in the cult or exclude Israelites from such participation. In their present context all these texts come together to form one overall teaching about Torah. The Decalogue now stands as a preamble to the collection, but is this text of early origin? It can be argued that ideas usually begin simply and are then expanded, but equally well a later writer can extract from complex matter a quick summary of basic points. Which is the better explanation of the Decalogue? The difficulty of producing one compelling answer to this issue highlights the difficulty which scholars have had in trying to trace the source of the legal material in the context of Israelite history.

E. W. Nicholson[4] has examined the major lines of thought on this matter produced by modern scholarship. G. Von Rad has suggested that the Sinai material was not originally connected with the historical theme of land settlement stemming from the exodus from Egypt but represents cultic traditions connected with coming before the Lord of Israel at a festival time to celebrate the tribal deity.[5] M. Noth, working on the origins of Israel, picked up Joshua 24 with its reference to a gathering of all the tribes at Shechem. Noth saw this as the occasion of a covenant renewal ceremony, linking together the federated tribes with their common God.[6] By contrast A. Weiser,[7] although agreeing that the Exodus and Sinai traditions emerged from a worship, festival setting, thought that the two traditions cannot be separated and formed part of the one liturgical event. The recital of God's acts with regard to the Israelites in Egypt provided the setting in cult for the people's agreement to the legal codes as an ongoing religious commitment.

The focus here is the theme of Covenant or contract. The laws of Israel make sense within the setting of the nation's agreement with its deity. This topic is highlighted, within the Torah, by the phrase 'an everlasting covenant' (*berit olam*). The first mention of such an idea is found in Genesis 9, where God sets out his future commitment to Noah, after the Flood. Later in Genesis the same phrase is used to define God's relationship with Abraham. But, whereas the same deity is involved in each case, the content of the contracts is different. To Noah the promise is that the world will not be destroyed again, the promise to Abraham has to do with an heir and with land. In the Sinai material the content is different again — this time the whole legal and cultic systems of Israel connected with the figure of Moses. Covenant, then, is not a simple or single concept. Nor is it clear whether the idea is an ancient one or one that the final editors used to bring together originally separate parts of Torah tradition.

Further light was shed on this topic by the work of G. E. Mendenhall, who pointed out the similarity of Israelite religious covenant to the form of political treaties in the ancient Near East.[8] Copies of treaties are still in existence dating from the second and first millennia BCE. Mendenhall argued that they have a common form:

- historical preamble, rehearsing the benefits accruing from the treaty in the past
- terms of the new form of the treaty
- sanctions for failure to keep to the alliance
- witness of deities of nations involved

The form of such treaties most relevant for the OT is that of a treaty between a sovereign ruler and a dependent vassal. This is because of the gap between God and humans; although God reveals himself to Israel and so creates a special relationship with this nation this is not one of equal to equal, especially in the Sinai material where God's presence on the mountain is awesome and terrifying.

Examining the book of Exodus with Mendenhall's theory in mind allows the reader to notice that the introduction to the whole Sinai section of the text is prefaced with a short treaty formula in Exodus 19:3ff. Here God reminds the nation of the benefits he has given to Israel in Egypt and offers them a new chance to become a holy nation and a royal priesthood if they will keep his statutes and ordinances. The full form of sanctions and witnessing is absent from this section of text, but the passage does resemble a treaty formula.

Is this thesis the answer to the question of the sources of the Sinai material, then? Can it be definitively stated that the God of Israel is a Treaty God? D. J. McCarthy[9] has shown that there are some difficulties with the hypothesis. Although most political treaties have some elements in common, there is no one type which can be defined as *the* treaty or covenant.[10] He turns to the biblical material next and argues that there too Mendenhall did not sufficiently regard the nature of texts involved. The Decalogue, for example, cannot be classified as such a form, since there are no sanctions and witnesses attached to the prescribed code of practice.[11]

In addition it should be noted that the covenant theme within the OT as a whole utilizes other human contracts to explain the religious commitment of God and Israel. Thus the book of Hosea bases its argument concerning the failure of the divine–human contract on the model of a marriage contract. In chapter 2 the words of the Lord to the people take the form of a bill of divorce on the grounds of adultery, whereas the next section of the text relates the remaking of a marriage between God, the people and the land.[12] The three major prophets (e.g. Isa 50; Jer 3; Ezek 16) also engage the theme of marriage infidelity and imaging God as a faithful husband slighted by his wife, Israel. Thus the theme of covenant in the OT must be viewed as larger than just political treaty material.

It is obvious, however, from the amount of material connected with the Sinai theme, that this is a highly significant topic for the final editors of the OT. As it stands the whole Sinaitic covenant is focused through the figure of Moses as mediator of Law. This is the climax of Torah described as the five books of Moses.[13] Moses acts as priest, prophet and lawgiver on the holy mountain, forming a bridge between heaven and earth in a manner which, in the ancient world, was usually the prerogative of kings. This presentation of Moses indicates the high value placed on his name in the post-exilic period when kingship had ended for Israel. As indicated in Chapter 3,[14] some scholars have argued for Moses as an historical figure who did indeed stand for a monotheistic religion. However, there is no evidence external to the OT which would compel the acceptance of this interpretation. What is certain is that the figure of Moses underwent much development in the post-biblical Jewish literature and had an effect on Christian writings also.[15]

The impression that the reader of the Sinai material gains is that both Moses himself and the Law which he mediated to Israel had a unique quality about them — an idea which is enhanced perhaps by the motif of God writing the Law on stone tablets in heaven and handing them to the Israelite leader in a heavenly setting. This motif implies, then, that the Law of Israel originated in the heavenly sphere and opens the possibility of regarding Torah as the presence of God among his people.[16] However, here too there are difficulties of interpretation. Scholars have argued around the theme of uniqueness. In what does it consist? A. Alt[17] thought that the answer was in legal forms. The law codes of Sinai are in two main formats:

- the form of 'Thou shalt (not)' (apodeictic)
- the form of 'If A occurs then do B' (casuistic)

The casuistic format has been shown to be one common to the ancient Near East. Comparable forms can be found in Babylonian, Hittite and Assyrian texts. Alt argued that the apodeictic format, seen in the Decalogue, was one unique to Israelite religion. But this argument has not survived the discovery that apodeictic forms are to be found in other ancient law codes.[18]

It would be possible to argue that the uniqueness lies in the overall tone of the Sinai texts, that of an order for society which requires justice, and so, a defence against social violence. But here, too, other codes of the ancient Near East convey the idea that justice stems from the national gods and is passed from them to human societies. Hammurabi's Code, for instance,[19] contains the belief that social order is part of world order and that the laws of Babylon have been revealed to Hammurabi by his patron deity. This focuses the argument for the uniqueness of Sinaitic law on the name of the particular deity who appeared on Mount Sinai.

This book will return again and again to the topic of mythology, as in this instance. There is a layer of metaphor in the OT which is deeply connected with mythological material and this closely surrounds the figure of the deity. In the Sinai story it is a god of power who appears at the mountain. The summit of the mountain is wreathed in clouds, thunder roars and lightning flashes. Anyone who comes close to the sacred site is in danger of death, except for Moses the people's representative. This is a continuation of the god who struck down the Egyptians, who parted the waters and sent pillars of cloud and fire to protect and guide the Israelites as they fled from Pharaoh.

The deity named here is YHWH, the Lord of Israel. But the features of the divine power are reminiscent of another deity, that of Ugaritic Baal. In Ugarit it is Baal who is the god of storm, the Cloud-rider. He has the power to contend with Sea (Yam) and Death (Mot) on behalf of the gods and so receives the reward of his own mountain palace on Mount Zaphon.[20] It was noted in Chapter 3 that the OT appears to run together the gods El and YHWH — or, at least, there is no hostility between these two figures evidenced in the text. The same is not true of Baal.

The Deuteronomistic history frequently refers to a contest between YHWH and Baal for the service of the Israelites. The story of Elijah, for instance, contains the scene of the prophetic contest of strength between adherents of Baal and Yahweh in which each side calls on its god to send fire from heaven on the altar of sacrifice (1 Kings 18). In the story YHWH wins the contest, so vindicating the worship given to him by Elijah. M. Smith has argued that these stories reflect a development of religious thought in which YHWH took on the functions of El as life-giver, a role played in Ugaritic thought by Baal.[21]

Originally the religion of the Syro-Palestinian region centred on El, but as culture and politics changed in the region so religious belief treated El as a less powerful figure and found newer, younger gods who could be called upon in human need. In Ugarit this is shown by the Baal texts; the OT has a form which brings together a strong El with a strong YHWH and considers Baal as the type of false deity. Presumably this reflects social reality in which the nations who were Baal worshippers were engaged in political struggles for local supremacy with the YHWH worshippers.

Such mythological concerns may seem very remote and marginal matters for a modern readership of the OT. European religion since the Enlightenment, it could be argued, no longer deals with myth, treating the word as a term to define that which is fantasy. This attitude, however, is not a good one on which to base consideration of the God of the OT. Recently J. J. Niehaus[22] has shown that the appearance of God on Sinai is intimately connected with the range of theophany material in ancient Near Eastern religion. In chapters 3 and 4 of his book Niehaus describes the relationship to the biblical tradition of Egyptian, Hittite, Mesopotamian and Canaanite theophany traditions. This account includes arguments asserting that pagan gods were viewed as kings with their own kingdoms who chose to make covenants with their chosen peoples.[23] The physical sign connected with a divine theophany was often a natural event such as thunder:

God thundered through the Garden of Eden after his man and woman sinned, he thundered atop Mount Sinai, he thundered before Elijah and Ezekiel, and he thundered from Mount Zion in eschatological glory. But God is not the only god who thundered. It was thought throughout the ancient near east that thunder was a holy utterance ... Sumerian, Hittite, Akkadian, Egyptian (Amarna), and Ugaritic evidence makes this clear.[24]

In this mythological setting there are, once again, signs that the God of Sinai is not unique — this time in the sense of being a god of storm-theophany. That which constitutes the uniqueness, therefore, may simply be the particular combination of parts in a whole image. Treaty, law, powers of god may all, on their own, be part of the wider continuity of religious thought in the ancient world. What creates the uniqueness is the total product of these individual elements. For the Torah, the Lord of Israel, the storm god, is the one who gives laws and underpins social order, who must, in turn, be worshipped by faithful followers of the Yahwistic religion.

This brings the reader back to the final level of the edited text. D. E. Gowan[25] has produced a modern study of the book of Exodus in which he explores the theology of the text by using the technique of commentary. He takes each separate section within the Exodus traditions and shows that it has its own contribution to make to the theology of the book. This study leaves aside vexed questions of earlier sources and the cutting up of text into small fragments as a method of establishing the message of the writers and editors. Instead it picks up and investigates topics such as

- the absence of God
- the numinous
- promise
- the divine destroyer
- the god of grace and glory

Each of these themes can be found in particular chapters of Exodus. Thus the absence of God occurs in the opening chapters which describe Israelite suffering in Egypt. In these scenes there is no reference to any action on the part of Israel's deity to counter Egyptian oppression. The numinous refers to the mysterious revelation of God to Moses in the desert. The divine destroyer is the image of the God of Israel which emerges in the actual exodus from Egypt with its long-drawn-out tale of contest of power between God and Pharaoh, climaxing in the retributive deaths of Egyptian children. The chapter on grace and glory treats the Sinaitic covenant. Gowan refers to this event as a gift, thus giving an insight into the caring nature of the deity:

The new relationship is thus a gift, and many interpreters of the Sinai Covenant have emphasised that. In the act of deliverance from Egypt, God had already cared for Israel before he asked any response from them.[26]

This gift is given an identity as commandment. God's love for us 'led him to give us the knowledge that he is our creator'[27] and then to give us the knowledge of our inequality with God so that we could govern our lives appropriately:

Once they had achieved self-awareness through evolution, and then an awareness of God through revelation... God gave them commandments. The commandments made it clear that this is not a relationship between equals, and they offered direction for the human will, which is supported at the human level neither by adequate wisdom nor by adequate goodness to keep them from making terrible mistakes.[28]

In each section of his study Gowan moves from the text of Exodus to the OT at large and then to Judaism and Christianity to show how the theology of the original text has been developed within a continuous tradition. His reflection on the tradition which emanates from the Sinai material touches on the themes of divine initiative–human response and the concept of nurturing love as the bond here.[29]

Gowan's study intends to make the text of Exodus accessible to the modern reader; it assumes a continuity at some level between the ancient readers of the OT, Christian and Jewish readers of the biblical books, and a twentieth-century readership. Not all commentators would agree that such a continuity of thought can validly be posited. R. Carroll, for instance, in *Wolf in the Sheepfold*,[30] argues that the subject of the OT law codes is controversial. He points out that Christian tradition shaped the OT to Christological purposes by treating it in an allegorical manner. This becomes problematical if combined with a literalistic reading of parts of the OT library. The Mosaic regulations helped to shape the nature of Second Temple Judaism but early Christian tradition threw out much of this system, 'baptism for circumcision, eucharist for passover, the death of Jesus in commemorative forms for sacrifice; dietary laws disappeared'.[31] However, the need for internal structures in early Christian communities appears to have led to a more literal reading of some parts of the OT legal material. Rules concerning daily life, such as the Decalogue, were reinstated while cultic law was omitted. This tradition has deceived many modern readers who assume that such a division between moral and ceremonial law is part of the OT itself. But this is not so; in the OT cultic law and moral law are intermingled and form a whole. Contemporary readers, in a world where Christian society appears to be collapsing, hanker after 'true Christian morality' and assume that the image of a god of law can achieve this end. Carroll argues that this is a mistaken way of reading the OT law texts:

A close reading of Leviticus will convince any modern reader of the pointlessness of trying to construct society today after the model of such regulations ... change them, update them ... and they become other than the historical regulations of a people living under the conditions of time and history.[32]

Times change, Carroll states, cultures change and the literal readings of ancient texts have to give way to new forms of reading.

D. J. Clines also doubts that the law codes of the OT reflect a universal message.[33] He approaches the material from the point of view of the ideology of writers and readers of the OT. He argues 'The Ten Commandments exist because it is in someone's interest for them to exist. In *whose* interest, then, are they?'[34]

Clines answers his own question by looking for the social context of the writers, which he believes to be that of the governing classes of the ancient world. He outlines the type of reader involved here as:

an individual, a male, an Israelite, employed, a house-owner, married, old enough to have working children but young enough to have living parents, living in a 'city', wealthy enough to possess an ox and an ass and slaves, important enough to be called to give evidence in a lawsuit.[35]

All this Clines deduces from the social and religious interests embodied in the ten clauses of the lawcode. The text, then, does not give voice to the poor, the widowed, or to women. Essentially it reflects the world-view of a certain social class and its interests. If, for instance, 'Do not kill' is addressed to blood feud concepts, the ones outlawing this practice

are the conservative fathers; for blood revenge makes for social instability, and the fathers stand for social cohesion and order; and they are the ones with power.[36]

Cline's approach would make the god of law and covenant the image of the deity held by the powerful class of an ancient society, a god who mirrors their attitudes and values. Is it possible, nonetheless, to argue for some wider relevance of this image of God to readers of the OT? The contribution of this particular image of God to the ideas of God in the OT has to do with a broader question than the value to be given to a particular law or to collections of law in law codes. The modern Western world has a tendency to regard laws as an evil which has to be tolerated for the sake of social peace. There is no great value in laws since they are restrictions on personal liberty; but there needs to be a check on murder and theft, for example. The image of God of law offers a critique on this attitude. The breadth of meaning of the word 'Torah' — from five books (Genesis to Deuteronomy), to law codes, to individual laws, to the whole teaching of self-identity to a reader — indicates the depth of meaning connected with this divine image.

The broadest setting of Sinai is the first chapter of Genesis, where God creates a good world through the principle of a rational and ordered plan, a word of command and the activity of ordering and separation. In line with the image of a creator god, the god of Sinai creates an ordered social universe for human beings. The divine command is now addressed to humans and the ordering and separating has to do with the particular items of codes of conduct both civil and religious.

It is possible to treat the law codes as the laws of an actual society, that of ancient Israel, and to envisage the manner in which the laws worked in such a society, as in the classic text of A. C. J. Phillips.[37] Recent scholars such as P. Davies who doubt that the OT details the life of historical Israel would have less enthusiasm for such a presentation.[38] But whether the OT describes an actual society or whether it offers a symbolic constitution,[39] it still offers points of vital interest for the modern reader. It is evidence for the belief that order is not evil, that control of action is not destruction of freedom, that social controls which work for the benefit of the whole community are indeed great gifts to human existence. Thus the OT gives a base for ethical codes which is rooted in the divine image itself.

It is possible, in this context, to view the Decalogue not simply as the main points of an ancient religious code, but rather as ongoing principles of human action. They are thus not just evidence for a long-past period but are points of natural law which pertain to any society, since they are rooted in the viability of human existence itself. The exact nature of detailed social laws drawn from this basis may be debated, but the belief that this debate is of value to human beings is thus endorsed.

The companion point to be made here is that of the value of mythology. It was stated above that the modern Western reader tends to find myth a difficult subject. But this is to misunderstand the function of myth in a society. Myth, usually found in narrative forms, explains for a society its origins and, by so doing, gives a sense of purpose to its citizens. The images connected with the storm god emphasize the power and authority of the deity. An electric storm kills and destroys, shattering trees and rocks with its charged force, but the after-effects of the rain are growth and fertility in the land. The storm god is thus a deity who controls the ultimate working out of life and death.

Modern Western society has generally preserved a belief in the value of having a concept of God. However, this has been accompanied by the abandonment of belief in the value of concepts of other supernatural beings such as angels and demons. The effect has been to cut the biblical God off from those phenomena which give depth and meaning to the divine. God can easily become a less than powerful figure and can, indeed, cease to be regarded as a 'being'. In this approach 'God' is the term for describing the combination of generous, patient and caring acts which hold together for good a human society.[40]

Yet M. Eliade[41] has argued that all societies have their myths of origin, even if these are not recognizably religious. Modern Britain may look back to great social reformers such as William Wilberforce, thus continuing the theme of heroes and heroines of the past much as in the Moses legends. Twentieth-century Spain may have had its religious focus in events such as the Holy Week Penitents and their processions, while Russia, in the same period, had its May Day parade of the armed might of the state, accompanied by the banners carrying the images of those who inspired the Revolution, but both societies were acting out rituals serving to inform citizens of the true meaning to be attached to their society.

The demythologizing of biblical ideas of God has left the area of myth to the anthropologists and to those Christian communities which have a conservative attitude to the biblical tradition. Niehaus's book fits into this category since it is part of a series of textbooks on aspects of OT theology which has been sponsored by an evangelical Bible college.[42] The individual focus of such a college results in the harmonizing of different strands of OT thought with a particular interpretation of Christian exegesis. Yet it is within the evangelical world-view that scholars are found who take the mythology of the OT seriously enough to research its background in thought in the ancient Near East, and who recognize the centrality of mythological images of God to the formation of OT concepts of the divine.

The combining of law as a rational component of social identity with the mythology of a storm god is the particular content of the image of the god of law and covenant to be found in the Sinai material. The significance of this view of the deity is given a further dimension in the last book of Torah, the book of Deuteronomy. The next chapter of this study turns to the developments of law, covenant and deity in that text.

Summary

The focus here is the material found in the OT between Exodus 19 and Numbers. This is largely legal material, dealing with the rules of conduct for civil and religious life in ancient Israel. The complexity of the component parts of these texts is dealt with and this paves the way for discussing the picture of God as making a contract with human beings. A further aspect of this material is the meeting of Israel and its Lord at Mount Sinai. This motif raises the question of the role of mythology in the OT ideas about the deity. Finally, scholarship relating to the universal value of the law codes is discussed.

Notes

1   The name of God in Exodus 3 is derived from the verb 'to be'. It is unclear, however, whether the verbal form used in the text should be translated as: 'I am who / what I am', 'I will be what I will be', or 'I cause to be that which is'. There has long been a scholarly debate on this topic. For a short account of this issue see R. Clifford, 'Exodus' in R. Brown, J. Fitzmyer and R. Murphy (eds), *The New Jerome Biblical Commentary* (Englewood Cliffs, NJ: Prentice-Hall/London: Geoffrey Chapman, 1989), pp. 46–7.
2   For an indication of the weight placed on this motif in Jewish tradition see *Wisdom of Solomon* 11, 17, 18.
3   A number of Psalms focus on the theme of Exodus. See e.g. Pss 114, 135, 136.
4   See E. W. Nicholson, *Exodus and Sinai in History and Tradition* (Oxford: Blackwell, 1973).

5   G. Von Rad's classic text, which includes this material, is *Old Testament Theology*, vols I and II (Edinburgh and London: Oliver & Boyd, 1962).

6   M. Noth's key work here is *The History of Israel* (2nd edn; London: A. & C. Black / New York: Harper and Row, 1960).

7   See A. Weiser, *Introduction to the Old Testament* (London: SCM Press, 1961).

8   See G. E. Mendenhall, 'Covenant forms in Israelite tradition', *Biblical Archaeologist* 17 (1954), pp. 50–76.

9   D. J. McCarthy, *Treaty and Covenant: A Study in Form in the Ancient Oriental Documents and the Old Testament* (Analecta Biblica 21; Rome, 1963).

10 Cf. Nicholson (1973), pp. 48–9.

11 Cf. Nicholson (1973), pp. 51–2.

12 The evidence for this statement is to be found in Hosea 2:16–23, where the prophet speaks of a new covenant / marriage alliance to be made between God and people. This will include not only the cessation of war and the firmer hold of justice in society but will link humans with all other animals and with the earth itself in a total system of beneficial interaction.

13 The Jewish tradition ascribes the first five books of the OT to Moses. This is likely to be legend, but it gives a certain significance to the overall meaning of the books of Torah. The different elements in these books (civic matters, cultic rules and so forth) are to be read together and viewed as the product of a single rational world-view. This in turn gives greater value to the function of law and order in mirroring divine character and as a vital undergirding to human society.

14 See above, pp. 26–7.

15 For more information on this issue see, e.g. M. E. Mills, *Human Agents of Cosmic Power in Hellenistic Judaism and the Synoptic Tradition* (Sheffield: Sheffield Academic Press, 1990), ch. 3.

16 See, for instance, the book of Sirach, in the Greek-language Jewish Wisdom texts, where the Law in Israel has become God-with-us: cf. Sir 24.

17 A. Alt, *Essays on Old Testament History and Religion* (Oxford: Blackwell, 1966), pp. 81–132.

18 More particularly in treaties in the ancient Near East. Cf. J. L. McKenzie, 'Aspects of Old Testament thought' in Brown, Fitzmyer and Murphy (eds), *The New Jerome Biblical Commentary*, p. 1299.

19 The Code of Hammurabi has become a classic piece of comparative evidence for OT law and covenant. Its text can be found in J. B. Pritchard (ed.), *Ancient Near Eastern Texts Relating to the Old Testament* (Princeton: Princeton University Press, 1969).

20 The source for this account is the Baal legends which have been unearthed in Ugarit (Ras Shamra), the texts of which are to be found in Pritchard (1969).

21 M. Smith, *The Early History of God* (New York: Harper & Row, 1990), ch. 2.

22 J. J. Niehaus, *God at Sinai* (Carlisle: Paternoster, 1995).

23 Niehaus (1995), pp. 84–93.

24 Niehaus (1995), p. 125.

25 D. E. Gowan, *Theology in Exodus* (Louisville: John Knox, 1994).

26 Gowan (1994), p. 176.

27 Gowan (1994), p. 177.

28 Gowan (1994), p. 179.

29 Gowan (1994), pp. 186–96.

30 R. P. Carroll, *Wolf in the Sheepfold* (London: SCM Press, 1997).

31 Carroll (1997), p. 75.
32 Carrol (1997), p. 77.
33 D. J. Clines, *Interested Parties: The Ideology of Writers and Readers of the Hebrew Bible* (Sheffield: Sheffield Academic Press, 1995), ch. 2.
34 Clines (1995), p. 32.
35 Clines (1995), pp. 33–4.
36 Clines (1995), p. 44.
37 A. C. J. Phillips, *Ancient Israel's Criminal Law* (Oxford: Blackwell, 1970).
38 See P. R. Davies, *In Search of Ancient Israel* (Sheffield: Sheffield Academic Press, 1990). The earlier chapters of this study outline the foundational stance of Davies referred to in this book.
39 What is meant by symbolic constitution here is that, even if these laws are not the complete legal system of Israel, or even if they do not represent at all what actually happened legally in ancient Israel, they do present the reader with a coherent picture of the foundation in law which underpins one society's identity. The legal structures offered by the text thus form a 'symbolic world' within whose boundaries the reader is invited to operate ideologically.
40 A fuller understanding of the issues involved here can be gained by reading, e.g., P. Vardy, *The Puzzle of God* (London: HarperCollins, 1990). An example of a non-realist interpretation of the concept of God can be found in the writings of the modern theologian Don Cupitt.
41 Cf. M. Eliade, *Myth and Reality* (New York: Harper & Row, 1963).
42 See here the preface to the series of OT Theology books produced by Trinity Evangelical Divinity School, as found in Niehaus (1995), pp. 11–12.

5 God of love and jealousy in Deuteronomy

The book of Deuteronomy provides the reader of the OT with another version of the Israelite religious traditions relating to a god of law and covenant. The title *Deuteros Nomos* (Second Law) reflects the section of the book which refers to the king of Israel having a copy of the law book at his side (Deut 17:18). It also, however, reflects the probable reaction of a reader who encounters this book having first read through the sections on law to be found in Exodus to Numbers. For such a reader Deuteronomy raises echoes of the legal codes which they have already met.

The book is structured around two main sections — an extended historical introduction in the first eleven chapters and the legal code of chapters 12 – 26. The legal material mirrors closely the codes of Exodus to Numbers but here are some significant differences. There is overall less connection with cultic, priestly concerns and more interest in the working of laws within a state setting.[1] In the Sinaitic Code, murder, for instance, was viewed as polluting the land since blood is a sacred substance. In the Deuteronomic Code, the focus is rather on the social effects of murder and how these will be dealt with.[2]

The introduction to the law section contains passages written in a sermon style and gives the broad context within which the laws should be interpreted. The whole book is woven together through the person of Moses, since the work is represented as his final speeches to the people of Israel before his death. Moses is thus able to look back at the ways in which God helped Israel from the exodus through the wandering in the desert and up till this last stage of Israel's sojourn in the wilderness. At the same time he can look forward to the future of Israelite settlement in the land of Canaan. Moses features here as the great ancestor whose moral advice supports his descendants across the centuries.[3]

The first part of the book contains a particular theological vocabulary which concentrates on certain key aspects of God's contract with Israel — a single deity makes an agreement with a particular nation — and this theological viewpoint is carried into the legal material also. Thus, for instance, the emphasis on the Lord of Israel as the people's only god is mirrored in the requirement of a central shrine where a single deity can be worshipped.[4] Although this theological attitude can be most easily seen in the introduction to the book, it can be traced also in the legal section of the text. The insistence on one Lord for Israel is partnered by the law of the central sanctuary and the tearing down of the shrines of other deities, for example.

The clear signs of Deuteronomy's individuality as a book means that it should not be read simply as an editing of the Sinaitic Code but should be viewed as a self-contained account of law and covenant with its own image of God. It is better to describe this unique identity in terms of a Deuteronomic language since the Deuteronomic pattern of theological thought can be found elsewhere in the OT, notably in the history books from Joshua to 2 Kings which follow the book of Deuteronomy in our Bibles. In this context Deuteronomy serves as the gathering together of the Torah and also as the introduction to the books of prophecy which reflect on Israelite fidelity to its deity once the land had been obtained. It is in this setting that the function of the book as a treaty text can be located.

The previous chapter touched on the issue of the connection between a god of law and covenant and ancient Near Eastern treaty formulas. This issue reappears in relation to Deuteronomy which scholars such as K. Baltzer[5] have described as shaped by such a treaty formula. It can be argued that the book of Deuteronomy lays down the terms of the alliance between the Lord and Israel and the histories show how Israel was unfaithful to that treaty, thus bringing about the fulfilment of the curses described by Moses in chapter 28. This is a useful idea in relation to the overall level of the editing together of the OT collection, but in relation to the nature of Deuteronomy itself it is less immediately helpful since this work, like the Decalogue, does not represent a 'pure' form of the political treaty structure.

Linked with this theme is the question of the origins of the book. It has long been asserted that Deuteronomy is connected with the account in 2 Kings of the finding of a law book in the Temple.[6] Scholarship has suggested that this law book is either the same work as Deuteronomy or an older version of the same law tradition. Most scholars accept a sixth-century date for the work as it is now shaped. It would be possible to argue that the law code at the heart of the book was originally separate from the present introduction. However, to come anywhere near a treaty form, the book needs the historical material at the beginning of the text as well as the code in the centre.

Deuteronomy is a work with its individual image of the deity, created under the heading of the theme of law and covenant. This deity is one who can be identified through human feelings of love and jealousy. It is possible, therefore, to identify in this book another OT image of God — that of the God of love and jealousy. The term 'love' is used in the text to refer to God's care for his people. The content of this term is the keeping faith with one's allies in a treaty. Typical of the language style is Moses's preaching in chapter 7. Here he states that God acted on behalf of his people because he loved them (verse 8) and he describes God as 'the faithful God who maintains covenant loyalty with those who love him' (verse 9). Although this is political language, it does not distance the deity from human beings but rather makes God seem intimately close, in constant careful supervision of what his people are experiencing. There is, however, a darker face to this image.

God cares for his people so much that he will give them a land. But this land is not empty, it already has inhabitants. The balance to God's love is that of his wrath which he will pour out on the Canaanites, thus driving them from the land in the face of the Israelite attack. Because there must be no temptation for Israel to worship other gods, the army must destroy all the women and children as well as breaking down cult centres. God, then, is both love and hate, it seems.

Moreover, God is jealous of his people. 'Jealousy' is a word which has negative connotations in human debate. It implies a possessiveness which is far from healthy and which can stifle its object. In Israel's past God has shown a proprietorial interest in their affairs. Thus Deuteronomy 4 reminds the reader of past rebellion against God, in the desert, and urges the future generations to take care not to rebel again, 'For the Lord your God is a devouring fire, a jealous God' (verse 24). Failure to follow this advice will lead to the destruction of Israel in the same manner in which the other nations have been destroyed: 'Like the nations that the Lord is destroying before you, so shall you perish, because you would not obey the voice of the Lord your God' (Deut 8:20). The term 'jealousy' covers both God's nurturing care and his fierce anger, uniting the two faces of the deity.

Within this theological vocabulary a particular strand of ideas about God emerges. This distinctive theology links together the topics of God and land, of Israel and land, of God and Israel. A concise summary of these themes can be found in a recent work by R. E. Clements.[7] Clements deals first with God, whose function the text highlights. There is only One Lord for Israel and the worship clauses of the Decalogue underline not only this truth but also the view that God cannot be adequately worshipped through statues and representations of the divine (the aniconic tradition). God requires a wholehearted service from his followers, so one central sanctuary will serve as a focus for worship. At this site it is the Name of the deity which resides and which represents God's indwelling of the Temple. In this context the Ark of the Lord is less a chariot-throne and more of a box for the safekeeping of holy objects.[8]

The doctrine of God is balanced by a doctrine of Israel. Israel is a nation[9] with a centralized government and a land of its own. The Lord of Israel is not only a national deity but stands as the real King or Suzerain of the nation. The human king referred to in chapter 17 is more of a philosopher-leader and law-interpreter than a world-class power figure. The focusing of power themes on the deity is carried through by two further themes in the book.[10] These are election and covenant. Election represents the idea that Israel did not have a particular deity by chance but because that deity sought the people out and chose to bless them for his own power and glory. The practical example of this is God's gift of the land.

But God's giving requires response from Israel. This is the setting for covenant. God is a great sovereign who has chosen to call a very weak nation into a highly beneficial alliance with himself. It is, therefore, the responsibility of the people to keep this alliance correctly. Covenant here means monolatry, worshipping only one god, and also socially just laws and guidelines. In Deuteronomy the three themes of God, people and land are woven together with the linking ideas of election, covenant and a just social order. It is this broader context which gives meaning to the language of love and jealousy.

The manner in which the thought of Deuteronomy forms a holistic code of language for Israelite society raises the question whether this book is intended to be a form of political constitution or whether it is a piece of theological reflection. A. D. H. Mayes asks:

Does it articulate a basis and framework for the political existence of a nation state, or is it a homiletical work designed to reform individual attitudes?[11]

On the surface the text describes the founding of a theocratic state in the plains of Moab. But the suggested date for the work, in the Persian period, offers a different interpretation: 'In Deuteronomy we have for the first time in Israel a theology, a reflective attempt to systematise belief.'[12] Thus it can be argued that the book intends to create a picture of social and religious identity, a picture rooted in past events which continue to shape present experience. The appearance of being a constitutional work is not totally misleading, since the text links together faith in a traditional god with particular forms of social living. The book serves, then, both as guidelines for daily existence and as a sermon on the nature of 'true religion'. If the origins of the present text reach back to Assyrian times then:

Deuteronomy ... expresses a systematically organised world view that revitalised

Israel's own tradition and so presented the Yahwistic option as a persuasive alternative within the uncertain and pluralist framework of late pre-exilic Judah.[13]

The image of a god of love and jealousy takes its meaning here from a social and political definition of Israelite identity. The language of emotion connects with the political through the particular form of love which is fidelity to one's political commitments, that is, *hesed*. In this context to be a good citizen is to honour the name or character of the patron god of one's society. God indeed becomes the good king who rewards loyal subjects with his own renewed promise of loyal support.

The overall coherence of thought is achieved through a particular set of terms and concepts. M. Weinfeld[14] has made a thorough search of the nature of Deuteronomistic language. He lists, in an appendix, the frequently occurring phrases and words. From this research it can be seen that 'love' is a term which applies primarily to God. The single nature of the Lord of Israel endows him with great power represented in the phrases 'with great might and outstretched arm' and 'greatness and strong hand'.[15] This power God has utilized for the benefit of Israel in freeing them from abject slavery in Egypt, a state described as a 'house of bondage' and 'an iron furnace'.[16] Therefore Israel now have God's Name among them, proving how his great power is at their service — 'the house / city which my name is called upon' and 'the site that the Lord will choose to make his name dwell there'.[17]

It is these vocabulary elements which give flesh to the idea of God's faithful love for his people. Through them the concept of a loving or faithful relationship of God and people is enunciated. 'Love' as a term controls other connected words — 'cleave to', 'fear', 'swear to', 'hearken to', 'obey the voice of', 'be perfect or blameless before him'.[18] This brings the reader to the reciprocal love and service which Israel owe their god.

When this reciprocal love is offered correctly the hand of the deity brings blessings, but failure on the people's part brings curses. Which leads on to the theme of wrath and anger. Love cannot be separated from this second feature, in Deuteronomy. It is love for Israel which leads YHWH to have anger against the nations who are to be exterminated. It is not specifically stated that the Canaanites are morally inferior to Israel; they are unlucky in their gods, though. These cannot stand up against YHWH's might.

Love and jealousy are closely related, however. If the Israelites fail to destroy all traces of alien culture in their midst they will themselves be the subject of their deity's awe-inspiring might. Deuteronomy 28 and 29 show the terror of this aspect of God's character in their detailed account of the horrors of a nation defeated and a land devastated. Future generations will see the devastation of that land and the afflictions with which the Lord has inflicted it — all its soil burnt out by sulphur and salt, nothing planted, nothing sprouting, unable to support any vegetation. (Deut 29:22–23)

God will wipe out his people just as he first wiped out the nations before them.

Which aspect of God's image, then, dominates this book — grace or judgement? J. G. McConville,[19] in a recent study, argues for the priority of a message made up from the interweaving of these two strands.[20] For McConville Deuteronomistic theology should not be described in terms of Deuteronomy alone but requires the consideration of those books which have the marks of being Deuteronomistic texts:

The Deuteronomistic achievement should not be under-estimated; it is nothing less than a theology of God and Israel on the plan of the nation's entire history, from the promises made of Abraham to the restoration from exile.[21]

The two strands of grace and judgement are woven together through all these events. In Deuteronomy the future of Israel is opened up in a fuller manner than has so far been revealed in the Torah. Two ways lie open before them in the land, the way of love of God, keeping his commandments, so blessing, and the way of infidelity, practising false worship, so cursing. Deuteronomy hints at the fact that both will occur: the blessing of a settlement of a good land, the creation of just rules and God-given leadership, followed by bad kings, unfaithful to covenant and law, whose ways bring invasion, deportation and loss for Israel. The future loss is not to be regarded as a sign of a vindictive deity, however, for the divine position is made clear at the start, at this time when the wanderings are nearly over and the settlement in the land is in sight. The freedom of human choice offered to Israel is what makes possible, even probable, curse as well as blessing.

'Grace in the end', though, is the conclusion McConville reaches. Chapter 30 of Deuteronomy shows the repentance of the people in exile and a renewal of their fortunes, with a return to the land.[22] God's love here takes a further step: beyond first love and failure of relationship lies a mercy which takes back to alliance a people now wiser if saddened. God will not abandon them forever: 'Deuteronomy will not abandon its commitment to the vision of a people in free and harmonious relationship with their God (30:8).'[23]

McConville's study thus focuses on the overarching continuity of God as love and faithfulness for Israel. Another recent work, that of T. Longman and D. G. Reid,[24] investigates the theme of holy warfare as a subordinate part of the God of love. The context for this theme is Deuteronomy's language of God's mighty arm, which provides an example of the concept of God as warrior whose covenantal care for Israel is that of a mighty general leading the Israelite army to victory. A triumphant army in the ancient Near East could validly claim the spoils. In holy war all must be offered to YHWH — all must be burnt or destroyed in God's name and so given to the deity.

Longman and Reid point to G. Von Rad[25] as a major twentieth-century contributor to the investigation of holy war. Their own contribution focuses less on war itself and more on the figure of God the divine warrior which this theme involves. The basis for their argument is the fact that all events of life are viewed as of religious significance in the OT. War is no exception. However, the OT singles out some Israelite battles for special status as events which occur through divine planning and initiation, a fact which guarantees Israelite success:

The central principle is that God is present in the battle with his people as a warrior. This is the origin of the divine warrior theme, the experience of God's presence in battle.[26]

The theme of the exodus from Egypt and the crossing of the sea is one major example of this, and the story of the Plagues in Egypt (Exod 7 – 12) contains many descriptions of the might of YHWH's hand or arm — a vocabulary repeated in the book of Deuteronomy and in Deuteronomistic thought. Holy war consists of clear stages:

- spiritual preparation
- weapons and numbers
- the march
- the combatants
- praise after battle
- the Ban (*herem*)

In all these stages God is present with his people; preparation therefore focuses on spiritual reflection just as completion offers the whole triumph back to God as source of victory:

Many of the acts that preceded a war in the Hebrew Bible indicate the religious nature of the conflict. Sacrifice, circumcision, vows, oracular enquiries, ritual cleanness — each of these elements announced Israel's understanding that God was present with them in battle.[27]

A successful campaign can thus be described as a 'Day of the Lord', made more literal by the texts which refer to Israel's carrying the Ark of the Lord at the head of their army:

The dual response to the appearance of the ark in the Israelite camp illustrates the ark's function and ancient Near Eastern perceptions of the role of the divine in warfare. The Israelites shouted out ... The Philistines reacted with fear.[28]

This Lord's day could be repeated endlessly in historical battles with each military event representing 'a day'. But in prophecy there is a shift from 'a day' to 'the Day of the Lord'. The Day represents the time when

God will judge Israel and Judah, allowing foreigners to take their land away. Beyond the disaster of the Babylonian Captivity lies a future Day — that of the Endtime when God will come in power to judge all nations in a final show of strength.

The origins of this holy war theme and the identity of YHWH as the divine warrior appear to lie in ancient mythology. In other ancient Near Eastern religions gods are shown to engage in a creation war.[29] In the OT God's first war involves a triumph over the waters of chaos — a theme barely visible in Genesis 1:1–3 but much more obvious in texts such as Psalm 29:10, Psalm 74:12–17. J. Day's study *God's Conflict with the Dragon and the Sea*[30] showed how much the OT echoes ancient Near Eastern thought-patterns on the subject of waters as a sign for chaos. It is not only creation which has traces of military metaphor, however. Psalm 77:16–20 draws history into the same thought-world by describing the exodus as a triumph by the Lord of Israel over the people's enemy, watery chaos.

Deuteronomy takes this historical aspect of warfare as the main frame for the alliance which God makes with his people. The image of a fierce, angry God in Deuteronomy can be viewed as yet another, and a major, example of the divine warrior concept of deity. The Lord of Israel will march at the head of his army, with his mighty hand and outstretched arm being those of a powerful warrior brandishing his weapons. The enemy troops will give way to Israel and their Lord; as a consequence all the fruits of victory will come back to God.

But this brings the reader back to an issue raised earlier in this chapter — that of the value of such an image for contemporary society. Mass media coverage of news items makes the modern reader aware that there is only too much 'ethnic cleansing' happening on the planet: from marsh Arabs in Iraq to Bosnians, Serbs and Croats in the Balkans, to competing tribes in African states. The connection between these modern events and the book of Deuteronomy is the Ban (*herem*). Under this rule all conquered peoples and their possessions are to be consecrated to God by an act of annihilation. W. Dietrich notes that

The mass of the little less than 80 occurrences of the HRM are found in the Deuteronomistic writings. Its writers liked ... to portray the taking of the land of Palestine by Israel as a victorious conquest.[31]

The language of annihilation can be balanced, however, by the fact that the Deuteronomistic writer

changed the rabid picture of the taking of the land in the Deuteronomistic book of Joshua; it says that Israel did not succeed in creating a tabula rasa; on the contrary, foreign tribes continued to live in the land.[32]

At the same time further evidence from the ancient Near East indicates that the destruction of peoples was part of the ancient thought-world. A

Moabite stone set up by King Mesha carries the information 'I killed all the peoples of the town as a sacrifice for Kamosh and for Moab. And I removed the altar of their Dod from there.'[33]

However, the fact remains that, as a religious text, Deuteronomy has an image of God which appears to encourage bloodthirsty behaviour in war. It seems possible that readers of the book may be encouraged to put the concept of the Ban into practice in their own day. It is certainly true that in the history of Christians and of Jews, two religions which take the Hebrew texts as inspired, there have been signs of such an effect. In the Christian Boer state in South Africa the thought-world of Deuteronomy provided inspiration for the displacement of native Africans from the land. In more recent Jewish history the Zionist movement has also sometimes laid claim to land in the face of Palestinian opposition on the grounds of a divine plan to give a promised land to chosen people.

Some balancing comments can be made here. McConville, like Dietrich, emphasizes the metaphorical nature of this language, pointing out that the idea of gods fighting as patrons of nations and driving out the peoples of other deities is a common mode in the literature of the ancient Near East.[34] It can also be argued that there is no definite archaeological evidence that Israel did in fact invade and destroy whole towns and settlements, even though there is indication that the Late Bronze Age was a period lacking in stability in Canaan, with the collapse of Egyptian hegemony.[35]

If the language of divine warfare is a matter of literary device, it can be argued that OT language is often vivid and strong. Since in fact life was extremely uncertain and survival a matter of effort, religious language could offer a sign that there is hope for the future, that one will not be constantly at risk from invaders. Writers of texts may have feared the worst but have made the most of possible victory, not in order to gloat over the fate of others, but to assert the continuity of their own national or social identity in a time when it was likely that it would be wiped out.

Yet the language of the text exists in its own right now and may be read by new audiences living in very different conditions. It remains a possibility that the book can lead to oppression as well as to freedom and responsibility. The image of a god of love and jealousy would here take a turn towards the darker aspect of the emotions. Attached to this problem is the broader one of the validity of using 'love' and 'jealousy' as proper images for God. These words are part of human language. In Deuteronomy 'love' translates *hesed*, a term for fidelity and loyalty rather than intimate connection. This is in keeping with the theme of political alliance which is a major shaping tool of the writer. However, the broader context of the book's message brings a more intimate note to the term 'love'. God is like a kinsman in the Exodus account. He intervenes to ransom his people, paying back the death of 'his' sons with the death of Egyptian children. Thus the language does not remain neutral, it slips into a more ordinary human mode, that of the family or kinship group. Also, jealousy is part of that love. But can such a term be applied to God? Readers will usually meet jealousy as a negative concept, an emotion destructive of social relations which should be avoided. Once again the immediate setting is the lofty theme of political treaty, but the broader context is the destruction of people who can be described as enemies of God.

The use of this emotive language to define the image of God in relationship to Israel humanizes the deity. God becomes more accessible since he can be described in language which already has meaning in human society. But such a humanizing lays the deity open to the charge of being too much akin to humans, sharing their darker side as well as their more constructive qualities. This theme will be touched on further when the language of husband and father is addressed as part of an investigation of the god of prophecy. It raises issues which are fiercely debated by some modern readers and which echo the difficulties of some early Christian readers of the OT such as Marcion[36] who would not have the OT as part of Christian reading since the deity it depicted was a flawed being.

Summary

In this chapter, one book, that of Deuteronomy, forms the central issue. Scholarship relating to the coherence of this book and its theology is addressed. The text appears to be well integrated but divergent images of God emerge — a deity at once loving and wrathful. A major critical point for modern readers is the divine demand for the annihilation of other nations along with their shrines, once the Israelites conquer the land. This leads to an investigation into the subject of Holy War in the OT.

Notes

1 E.g. R. E. Clements, *Deuteronomy* (Sheffield: Sheffield Academic Press, 1989), pp. 23–7.
2 E.g. Clements (1989), p. 25.
3 This is in line with the Testament genre of literature of which a number of

examples from the Graeco-Roman world have survived. See J. Charlesworth (ed.), *The Old Testament Pseudepigrapha*, vols 1–2 (London: Darton, Longman & Todd / New York: Doubleday, 1983, 1985) for English translations of Testament texts.

4   For a treatment of the link between law and theology in Deuteronomy see J. G. McConville, *Law and Theology in Deuteronomy* (Sheffield: Sheffield Academic Press, 1984).

5   K. Baltzer, *The Covenant Formulary* (Oxford: Blackwell, 1971).

6   This argument was initiated by W. M. L. de Wette in his study of 1805. It has since become the staple core of scholarly discussions of the origin of the book. For an account of the history of interpretation of this theme see, e.g., J. G. McConville, *Grace in the End* (Carlisle: Paternoster, 1993), ch. 2.

7   See note 1 above.

8   The descriptions of the Ark vary in the OT. It sometimes appears to be a throne, and yet in the Deuteronomic versions of Israelite tradition it is a chest in which the stone tablets of the Law can be kept and carried around with the people in their wanderings.

9   Clements (1989), p. 55.

10   Clements (1989), p. 56.

11   A. D. H. Mayes, 'On describing the purpose of Deuteronomy' in J. Rogerson (ed.), *The Pentateuch* (Sheffield: Sheffield Academic Press, 1996), p. 224.

12   Mayes (1996), p. 239.

13   Mayes (1996), p. 240.

14   M. Weinfeld, *Deuteronomy and the Deuteronomic School* (Oxford: Clarendon Press, 1972).

15   Weinfeld (1972), p. 329.

16   Weinfeld (1972), pp. 326–7.

17   Weinfeld (1972), p. 325.

18   Weinfeld (1972), p. 83.

19   McConville (1993).

20   McConville (1993), p. 64.

21   McConville (1993), p. 123.

22   McConville (1993), p. 136.

23   McConville (1993), p. 137.

24   Tremper Longman III and D. G. Reid, *God Is a Warrior* (Carlisle: Paternoster, 1995).

25   G. Von Rad, *Holy War in Ancient Israel* (Grand Rapids: Eerdmans, 1958).

26   Longman and Reid (1995), p.47.

27   Longman and Reid (1995), p. 37.

28   Longman and Reid (1995), pp. 49–52.

29   Longman and Reid (1995), pp. 83–5.

30   J. Day, *God's Conflict with the Dragon and the Sea* (Cambridge: Cambridge University Press, 1985).

31   W. Dietrich, 'The "ban" in the age of the early kings' in V. Fritz and P. R. Davies (eds), *The Origins of the Ancient Israelite States* (Sheffield: Sheffield Academic Press, 1996), p. 197.

32   Dietrich (1996), p. 198.

33   Dietrich (1996), p. 202.

34   See McConville (1993), pp. 139–40.

35   This opinion is based on the view that the Amarna Letters reflect the state of

Canaan at this time. The letters, which were excavated in Egypt, are evidence of an unstable political climate in the region. For a recent account of the social structures of early Israel in the area see N. P. Lemche, 'From patronage society to patronage society' in Fritz and Davies (eds) (1996).

36 Marcion was a second-century Christian who advocated the use of only ten Pauline epistles and Luke. He rejected the OT texts entirely as a valid source for Christian theology. His ideas were rejected by the Church at large, which kept in use the Hebrew texts, making them fit to Christian theology by looking for signposts to Christian beliefs within the older texts.

Section B
Prophecy

6 God as First and Last in Isaiah

Although the OT is a collection of books produced by different writers with individual interests, these books have been edited together in such a manner that each can be read as offering comment on the others. This style of exegesis can be labelled 'canonical criticism', since its basis is the existence of a corporate collection of texts (canon) subdivided into three sections of Law, Prophets and Writings.[1] The first five books of the OT (Torah) have the function of establishing a basis for the religious traditions of Yahwism; the next part of the collection, that of Prophecy, offers the reader a commentary on how the foundational concepts laid out in Law apply in history. In this context the term 'history' describes the events which occurred once Israel had entered the land which divine initiative was offering them. Establishment of the nation led to the popular demand for a king, according to the biblical account, and the prophets are situated in the times of kings of Israel and Judah, for the main part. Their message is a critique of the politics and culture of monarchical times, a critique offered in the name of the god first introduced to the reader in Torah and associated with the idea of alliance and patronage of a people.

The book of Isaiah is no exception here. The oracles recorded in the text are said by its editor to be the work of a Judahite prophet, Isaiah son of Amoz (Isa 1:1). However, scholars have long suggested that there are at least two writers to be considered – the earlier Judahite figure and a later, exilic author.[2] This suggestion takes into account the variety of mood within the book. Whereas the first 39 chapters tell mainly of judgement and doom, chapter 40 begins a new theme, that of comfort and consolation. Although there are signs that the final editing of the text has woven themes of hope into first Isaiah[3] and themes of doom into second Isaiah,[4] it is possible to isolate the second part of the book, from chapter 40 onwards, and to consider its contribution to the images of God in the OT.

In this section of the work there appears to be a consistency of language and attitude. The theme is one of comfort for God's people, a comfort which entails returning to a land of origin and which is brought about by the deity. The Lord of Israel features in these chapters as the only supreme deity and is referred to by a number of titles — First and Last being the key title. By contrast to the Lord of Israel, the gods of Babylon are but lifeless statues with no power to affect human destiny.

The context for this message in the book of Isaiah is national history. In the language of the major prophets[5] the invasions of Israel by Assyria and of Judah by Babylonia are not described in secular terms as invasion, deportation of peoples and economic decline. Instead they are given a theological frame of reference: invasion is judgement caused by the nation's sin, deportation is the Exile, the land becomes a wilderness.[6] The first part of Isaiah shares this language code with other prophetic texts and can thus be described as a pre-exilic work. Chapters 40 onwards, however, appear to offer encouragement after the invasions have occurred. This has led scholars to label this section of the text 'the book of consolation' and to regard it as the product of the exilic and post-exilic ages.

It is necessary to account for the difference of approach to the image of the deity in the two main subsections of Isaiah. Although invasion and defeat are regarded as the work of God as judge and justified by divine authority to discipline a people who have strayed from God's commandments, the conquest of the nation by foreign powers raises some important religious questions which amount to a crisis of faith. How in fact *did* the foreigners triumph? Was it because of Israel's God being on the invaders' side or was it because of the superior power of the gods of the victorious nation? This second possibility, however, means that the Lord of Israel either cannot or will not defend his people. Such a deity is useless and the temptation, in the ancient Near East, would have been to adopt the gods of the opposing nation as one's own deity. For Isaiah's contemporaries this would have meant changing to a belief in Marduk, the chief Babylonian deity. The ancestral faith stands in danger of complete collapse. It is this crisis which the writer of second Isaiah appears to address.

The prophet has two tasks on hand: to reassure the people who have been deported that their cause is not lost, and to re-contextualize the ancestral deity in a setting of national disaster.

With regard to the first task, a message of doom and punishment is no longer appropriate. National defeat fulfils the prophecy of pre-exilic times. Is there no more to be said? Second Isaiah bridges the message of judgement into oracles of hope and salvation via the opening of chapter 40:

Comfort, comfort my people, says your God. Speak tenderly to Jerusalem, and cry to her ... that her iniquity is pardoned, that she has received from the Lord's hand double for all her sins. (Isa 40:2)

The national deity is thus transformed from a god of judgement to a god of redemption. Instead of destruction Jerusalem will experience rebuilding, instead of depopulation the land will experience a stream, an army, of exiles returning home.[7] In order to convey this message forcefully the prophet utilizes imagery which is already familiar to readers of the OT, drawn from themes of creation and exodus.

C. Stuhlmueller's study of *Creative Redemption in Deutero-Isaiah* dealt extensively with the theme of creation language in this book.[8] Stuhlmueller argued that the theology of the book links together creation and redemption. The term 'redeemer' (*goel*) is to be read in connection with YHWH's address to Israel as 'my son'.[9] God becomes the kinsman of the nation, a figure of tenderness and mercy. On to this base of redemption language is grafted the further image of God the creator.

The first creation is viewed by the prophet as a sign pointing to the fulfilment of creation themes in the refounding of the nation after the Exile. The text refers to the first creation as the former things, thus 'the former things I declared long ago ... suddenly I did them and they came to pass' (Isa 48:3). The past is not finished, however, since it leads to new things: 'From this time forward I make you hear new things ... They are created now, not long ago' (Isa 48:6–7).

Poetic language which describes the founding of a cosmos, a universe, is reused in the context of world history. In this extended application the founding spoken of is that of a new nation of Israel, brought back from exile. This is to be a new and unexpected event, but it is still the work of the ancient national deity. So Isaiah 48:13 makes a familiar deity speak to a new generation, one who 'laid the foundation of the earth' and 'spread out the heavens'. The term 'creation' (*bara*) is itself used sixteen times in the book,[10] referring only once to Adam but twelve times to Israel.

It was stated above that the focus of creation language is that of redemption. The term *goel* refers to a protective kinsman. One of the tasks such a kinsman could perform was that of marriage: marriage with a bereaved woman, a lonely widow who is to be married by the nearest kinsman and so made capable of bringing up children for her late husband. Second Isaiah uses this human social network to define the future security of Israel who will be married with her deity. The children so produced are, metaphorically, the remnant of faithful Jews who come back from exile to reclaim the land.

surely now you will be too crowded for your inhabitants ... Then you will say in your heart ... I was bereaved and barren, exiled and put away — so who has reared these? (Isa 49:19–21)

Stuhlmueller suggests that this calling into being of a new nation is paralleled with the calling into existence of the stars, in the first creation.[11] Thus creation and redemption are formed into one continuous poetic message for the reader.

The second theological topic which is a major part of second Isaiah's thought is that of the exodus. R. N. Whybray has given a succinct account of the Isaianic use of exodus themes in a recent commentary.[12] He argues that 'the period of Israel's history from which Deutero-Isaiah most frequently drew lessons was that of Israel's beginnings'.[13] In line with this theme the prophet introduces a number of supporting themes taken from the Torah accounts of the first exodus:

• hurried departure for the homeland
• the pillar of cloud
• divine intervention at the sea
• divine guidance in the journey through the wilderness
• YHWH's glory and its effect on the beholders[14]

The return to the land will be a new exodus and a new settlement. This time the people will stream from Babylonia rather than Egypt and they will take over again the land of settlement promised to them by God. But whereas the first events of founding a nation took place under pressure from neighbouring peoples, the Israelites chased by Egyptians and then fighting to claim the land, the new settlement will be a measured and ceremonial entry under the auspices of the Persian ruler, Cyrus. Under his patronage there will be no need to fight for territory since it has already been apportioned to the returnees by the imperial ruler and he will oversee its realization:

Thus says the Lord God: I will soon lift up my hand to the nations ... and they shall bring your sons in their bosom, and your daughters shall be carried on their shoulders. (Isa 49:22)

A further dimension is given to this material by the manner in which the prophet overlays the topics of creation and exodus with a particular approach to the nature of the deity. At critical points the text has YHWH speak in his own voice and define himself by a number of titles. One of these titles has already been referred to — that of the loving redeemer whose desire it is to bring Israel to safety. There are, however, a number of other titles used by Isaiah — such as Lord of Hosts and Holy One. Thus God states in chapter 43 that he is 'the Lord, your Holy One' (verse 15) and in chapter 48 the prophet proclaims of YHWH that 'the Lord of Hosts is his name' (verse 2). Just as with the themes of creation and exodus so with the divine titles, the ancient writer appears to make a deliberate re-use of traditional religious concepts.

The Lord of Hosts is a translation of the title *YHWH Sabaoth*. This title has a warfare basis. The Hosts are the divine army, either stars or angels elsewhere in the OT.[15] God is a great warrior leading his army to victory in a form of holy war.[16] Chapter 42 says of the Lord of Israel that he

goes forth like a soldier, like a warrior he stirs up his fury; he cries out, he shouts aloud, he shows himself mighty against his foes. (v. 13)

This divine warrior image of God is visible in Torah and in Psalms as well as in prophecy. It is one of the key images of God in the OT. In Isaiah it serves to define a god who punishes his people, as well as, here, a god whose power is used on his people's behalf.

Holy One also has a history of usage elsewhere in the OT. In Isaiah itself the term is used in the threefold acclamation of the deity in chapter 6. It is a title which describes the separate nature of God. In the cultic, priestly texts of the OT it is the otherness of God which requires people and objects used in the divine presence to be consecrated or set aside for that purpose.[17] This produces the secondary referent of 'holy' — the holiness of human existence which is dedicated to the deity. Other texts add to the range of meaning carried by the title Holy One. In the books of Amos and Ezekiel, for instance, it is associated with the splendour of God and the manifestation of his strength.

The prophet's combination of titles brings together images of God which are scattered across the OT and consciously applies them all to the same deity. A further title increases the impact of this theological device — the name First and Last. This title undergirds all the rest and gives them a special value. Only one deity deserves all these titles, only one deity is redeemer, holy, Lord of Hosts. The concept of monotheism is clearly in evidence in this approach to God. Thus the prophet refers to YHWH's sovereignty in chapter 40 of the book: 'The Lord is the everlasting God' (verse 28) and 'It is he who sits above the circle of the earth' (verse 22). In chapter 44 YHWH claims that he is 'the Lord, who made all things, who alone stretched out the heavens' (verse 24) and that 'I am the first and the last; besides me there is no god' (verse 6).

The historical context of this language has been referred to above; it is that of the crisis of belief in a national deity caused by military defeat. In exile it would be easy to turn to foreign deities and abandon ancestral beliefs. A way of preventing this is to turn events on their head. Far from being defeated by other gods, YHWH is the only God and it is he who determines the fates of all the nations. Second Isaiah deals with this theological matter both by ridiculing the other gods and by provocatively claiming Cyrus as a 'Davidic king' chosen to bring peace to Israel.

The caricaturing of the gods comes at regular intervals in the book and is first introduced in chapter 40 where the prophet asks, in the divine name, to what can YHWH be likened. Fun is then made of idols, cult statues of gods whose mouths cannot speak and whose ears cannot hear (verses 18–20). The same language occurs again at intervals and forms the setting for the trial of the other gods by YHWH. When the Jews watched Babylonian festival processions of the statues of Marduk and the lesser deities they were not seeing divine beings but human artefacts, states the prophet.[18]

The second part of the claim that YHWH is the universal deity comes in the passages where God points out that he has chosen Cyrus especially to be shepherd and ruler of his people and to lead them back to their land. A typical example of this theme is to be found in chapter 45 where the text reports YHWH speaking to Cyrus as his 'anointed', a title used in Psalm 132, for instance, for the Davidic line of kings. The purpose of this choice is so that 'he shall build my city and set my exiles free' (45:13). This is sensational ideology since foreign nations are usually viewed as hostile to Israel and as the enemy, as in Psalm 2, for instance. But now these nations are subordinate to the power of YHWH who uses them both to break down and to build up his chosen nation.

The manner of presentation of this theme in the Isaianic material gives a special significance to the relation between Israel and Persia which uniquely favours Israel over all Persian provinces. G. Garbini, however, has argued that this focus is not historically what happened; there was no special favour to one small province in the Empire.[19] Rather this manner of operating was a part of everyday practice for the Persian rulers. The re-settlement of an under-used region, focused on the renewing of its local religion, was a common tool of imperial policy. The secular term for this economic device would be 'colonization'. In second Isaiah, by contrast, the ordinariness of the return is played down and its religious significance as the working out of a mysterious, but ultimately benevolent, divine purpose, is emphasized.

For the reader of this book a deeper religious issue arises from its theological messages about politics and society in the Persian period, that of the possibility that second Isaiah marks a new development in Yahwistic tradition. In this new phase of religious belief there is a shift from worship of a single deity within the context of polytheism to a specifically monotheistic understanding of God. Recent scholarship has given a focus to this approach, seeing the text of second Isaiah not so much as clear evidence of an ongoing monotheistic religion, but rather as marking a new development which took place in the Persian period, when the Israelites had become Jews.[20] In this perspective the prophet has deliberately brought together a variety of ideas under the image of a single deity, God the First and the Last. All Israelite history can then be viewed as part of one single historical plan in which exodus foreshadows the return from the Exile. All the titles and names of the deity can equally be defined as parallel ways of calling upon the one single Lord of Israel. By claiming Cyrus as a Davidic king for Israel the author goes further than describing one God for Israel (henotheism) and argues that there is only one universal God, the Lord of Israel who alone was the First and will be the Last, thus bringing the destinies of other nations under the same divine plan and revealing the true worth of foreign gods as nothingness.

G. Garbini, writing on the origin and development of Yahwism,[21] argues that the historical roots of OT religious views lie with the resettlement of Judah:

It is ... at this moment and in this way that Yahwism was founded, projecting on to a period that we calculate to be around 1200 BC the situation existing in the second year of Darius.[22]

The sixth-century writers reshaped the nature and identity of the local deity, YHWH. Insofar as archaeological research reflects the nature of religious beliefs in Syro-Palestine of an earlier period, it illustrates a complex relationship between various deities worshipped by the local inhabitants:

the texts show a divine figure [YHWH] worshipped in the region of Syria and Palestine from the beginning of the second millennium BC on, both by sedentary people and by nomads: a divine figure connected with the local pantheon but in no way pre-eminent.[23]

Further evidence is found among the many female figurines which have been excavated and in the representation of YHWH and his consort, his Asherah, excavated at Kuntillet Arjud,[24] of the diverse pantheon of gods revered in the first millennium BCE in the Palestinian region. In this setting an Israelite focus on YHWH as a national deity was no different from the forms of henotheistic worship practised by other small nations in the area.

But the final level of religious ideology in the OT has a different feel. In this editorial layer there is an exclusivism, only one deity and his one chosen people. This conceptual frame fits better with the world of the exiles of Yehud than with that of several centuries earlier. The book on *The Triumph of Elohim*, edited by D. Edelman,[25] offers the reader some further understanding of this topic. Its earlier chapters contain an account of a possible pantheon of Judaean religion by L. K. Handy[26] together with a chapter on the rise of YHWH in Israelite religion by H. Niehr. In later chapters P. R. Davies and T. L. Thompson[27] discuss the relationship between the development of Yahwism and the Persian / Greek time periods.

Davies begins by tackling the subject of 'Judaism' itself. He argues that this term is generally taken to mean a systematic body of ideas and practices as evidenced by modern Rabbinic Judaism, and which views itself as founded upon sacred books. However, it would be an anachronism to suggest that this sort of religious system existed in the sixth century. Nor should one view the Yahwism of the sixth century as a stage on the way to the inevitable and final form of Judaism. Rather the religious ideas of Jews in the sixth century should be viewed as an independent entity. In such a context there is not one Judaism, in whatever shape, but many judaisms. The OT is not all the Jewish literature of this time period which is extant and it was not seen, at the time, as *the* means of defining a religion.

The earliest possible traces of the creation of a body of sacred literature which records a religion are to be found in a text such as Sirach, the work of Ben Sira, composed at the end of the third century BCE. Ben Sira is aware of the Law and has a consistent approach to religion, based on Temple and priesthood, which he shares with his educated contemporaries. Yet there is no evidence that the traditions he refers to are the same reality as the present OT books, gathered in a single collection. What the scribe and teacher knows of is material in the process of development.

A further stage in this growth of written forms of tradition is reached with the Hellenistic period. At this point Palestinian Jews had to decide whether to ally themselves with the Syrian Seleucid dynasty in its putting on of Greek culture and religion or to refuse co-operation. The result was civil war — a war in which the victors claimed victory for the Jewish cause. The feast of Dedication marks the belief that an alien religious culture had been destroyed and an ancestral faith upheld. Yet, for all that, the Hasmonean rulers were marked by living in a Graeco-Roman world. The homes of the upper-class priests which were destroyed in the Jewish War of the first century CE, which have been excavated, show a mixture of Greek and Jewish furnishing.[28] Part of this influence was the need to demonstrate the ancient roots of tradition, evidenced by a library of religious works. Davies has previously argued this interpretation of the origins of the OT in his work *In Search of Ancient Israel*.[29] The Hellenistic period, then, probably marks the beginning of the OT as it has come down to the modern period.[30]

The OT, in this theory, reflects the religious views of the third century BCE / first century CE, with traces of an older sixth-century perspective. Thompson's chapter complements this account. He argues that the exclusive monotheism found in the latest levels of the OT comes from a time when Yahwism had to defend itself against syncretism, the harmonizing of one religion with another, which was part of Hellenistic culture. He says:

The need to reject syncretism and the dominance of Greek culture in *exclusive* monotheistic terms created a need to affirm the indigenous tradition of *inclusive* monotheism in *exclusivistic anti-Hellenistic terms*.[31]

This is the final stage of a longer developmental pattern in the ancient Near East. Thompson suggests that by the sixth century BCE ancient religions were moving from polytheism to monotheism. This can be traced in Greek religion where tales of divine exploits brought ridicule on the divine among educated people, who turned instead to the schools of philosophy for an account of the world and its principles. In Asia also there was a movement from polytheism to a belief in a single divine power, taking place from the time of the Persian Empire:

In contrast to the Greek historians, philosophers and playwrights, the intellectuals of Asia chose not to reject but to affirm the traditions of the past as expressions of true reality ... Inclusive monotheism is not primarily antagonistic towards polytheism; instead it interprets and restructures it.[32]

The OT reveals that its authors were part of this cultural environment. The fact that the texts of the OT refer to a single god, YHWH, by a plural referent, Elohim, is evidence of these transitions in belief. If the earliest level of religion in Syro-Palestine knew El as a single deity and YHWH as another divine figure, the latest stages of development re-applied the word 'El', now meaning 'gods', to the name YHWH, subordinating the plural to the singular. The truer translation of Elohim here would be 'Divinity' or what modern readers usually understand by the term 'God'.

A further article by Thompson, published in 1935,[33] develops these arguments by showing how a key passage, that of the scene of Moses and the burning bush, bears traces of the development of Yahwism. In Exodus 3 the deity is referred to both as YHWH and as Elohim. The text makes a self-conscious effort to link YHWH of Israel with the El of the fathers. In the past God revealed himself in the form of El but now he reveals himself in his true form, that of YHWH. This is not a movement against polytheism so much as a refining of this religious attitude which can be described as inclusive monotheism. It accommodates several parallel deities by subsuming them under one particular name. Thompson suggests that this was a stage in the development of Yahwism prior to the final stage of exclusive monotheism. It belongs to the period of the fourth to the second centuries BCE, roughly during the existence of the Persian Empire. The text of Exodus 3

legitimizes and identifies the gods of the patriarchal stories and of Israel's ancestors as truly expressive of the divine ... in bringing these elements together, the story accomplishes the emotional task of identifying the divine possessively: their god — the god of their forgotten tradition — is God himself.[34]

As the reader will recall from an earlier chapter, not all scholars accept the line of argument produced by Davies, Thompson and the students of ancient Near Eastern comparative religion, such as M. Smith, concerning the late date of OT monotheism. However, these arguments deserve consideration. There is, for example, a distinction in biblical text between

Deuteronomy, which states that Israel must not worship other gods, and second Isaiah which argues that the other gods are nothing, being empty and lifeless objects created for human use. The texts themselves, then, invite the reader to a deeper evaluation of the religious views expressed therein.

It is possible to argue that second Isaiah is evidence for the development of new ideas about the image of God in the OT. Within the shape of the canonical collection of a fixed set of texts, it may even be said that the prophet invented monotheism. In the historical context offered by Isaiah this would be the result of an enormous political, economic and social upheaval leading to a religious crisis. If the patron deity of a nation allows it to be defeated, is this because the deity is not strong enough to defend his country against other nations favoured by different and more powerful gods? A strong way of countering this view is to go in the opposite direction and to claim that defeat is part of the divine plan which, in the fullness of time, will lead to restitution of land. Something similar happens in the New Testament, with the death of Jesus of Nazareth converted into the climax of his power and authority and of his ability to re-unite worshippers with their god. The move to a 'God alone' theology is, perhaps, most clearly and fully represented in the image of God as First and Last. Such a deity is without parent and outlasts all other beings — this is the essence of a universal God, the proper foundation for the monotheistic approach to religious belief.

Summary

Attention now turns from Torah to Prophecy. Isaiah 40 is usually regarded by scholars as the start of a Second Book of Isaiah, written in the setting of the Babylonian Captivity of Judah and its inhabitants. This text appears to be strongly monotheistic in tone, applying titles such as First and Last to the Lord of Israel. The nature of this material is outlined and this moves into a discussion of the issue of development of religious thought in the OT: a literary feature which echoes the real-life shifts in understanding among the writers of its books. This chapter is the foil to Chapter 3, which brought out the possible polytheistic elements of the OT.

Notes

1   'Canonical criticism' refers to one particular style of commenting on the OT, in
    which the texts are considered in relation to their ultimate common

membership of the OT as an authoritative collection of texts for religious purposes. This style of criticism is associated with the scholar B. Childs.

2   Although the entire book is attributed to one named figure, Isaiah, it is unlikely that all parts of the book were written by the same person. The second part is attributed to a different writer and a later date than the earlier chapters, but no name can be given to the second writer, who may have preferred to operate anonymously, identifying himself with the memory of an older figure.

3   As, for instance, in Isaiah 11.

4   As, for instance, in Isaiah 42:18ff.

5   By major prophets is meant the three books of Isaiah, Jeremiah, Ezekiel.

6   For an example of invasion presented as divine punishment see Ezekiel 5:5ff.

7   See, for instance, Isaiah 43:1–7.

8   C. Stuhlmueller, *Creative Redemption in Deutero-Isaiah* (Rome: Gregorian University Press, 1970).

9   Stuhlmueller (1970), p. 105.

10   Cf. Stuhlmueller (1970), ch. 9.

11   Stuhlmueller (1970), pp. 184–5.

12   R. N. Whybray, *The Second Isaiah* (Sheffield: Sheffield Academic Press, 1983).

13   Whybray (1983), p. 49.

14   Whybray (1983), pp. 49–51.

15   See, for instance, Psalm 148, which combines the theme of angel host (verse 2) with that of stars (verse 3).

16   See, for instance, Psalm 80. See also Chapter 5 on Deuteronomy, in this book.

17   For an expansion of this topic see the article 'Holy' in J. B. Bauer (ed.), *Encyclopaedia of Biblical Theology* (London: Sheed & Ward, 4th edn, 1982), vol. 1, p. 372.

18   It is necessary to set a text such as that of Isa 44:9–20 in the context of a religious festival such as the annual processions for Marduk, held in Babylon.

19   Cf. G. Garbini, *History and Ideology in Ancient Israel* (London: SCM Press, 1988), pp. 93–4.

20   The texts of the OT describe YHWH's people as Israelites, in the time of the kings, but the book of Daniel knows their inheritors as Jews. This change of nomenclature marks the radical break which separates the nation of ancient Israel from the Persian province of Yehud. It leads the reader to consider carefully just how much continuity there was historically and culturally between these two societies.

21   Garbini (1988), ch. 4.

22   Garbini (1988), p. 64.

23   Garbini (1988), p. 57.

24   Garbini (1988), pp. 59–60.

25   D. V. Edelman (ed.), *The Triumph of Elohim* (Kampen: Kok Pharos, 1995).

26   See ch. 1 of Edelman's book and also the chapter on the patriarchal god in this book, where some of Handy's work is referred to.

27   See chs 4 and 6 of the Edelman book.

28   This is a reference to the Herodian houses which have been excavated in the Jewish Quarter of Jerusalem, just above the western wall, and are open to visitors to the city.

29   P. R. Davies, *In Search of Ancient Israel* (Sheffield: Sheffield Academic Press, 1992).

30   P. R. Davies in Edelman (ed.) (1995), p. 178.

31   T. L. Thompson, 'The intellectual matrix of early biblical narrative: inclusive monotheism in Persian period Palestine' in Edelman (ed.) (1995), p. 124.
32   Thompson (1995), pp. 115–16.
33   T. L. Thompson, 'How Yahweh became God: Exodus 3 and 6 and the heart of the Pentateuch', *Journal for the Study of the Old Testament* 68 (1995), pp. 57–74.
34   Ibid., p. 70.

7 God as father and husband in prophecy

As well as examining single books of prophecy for their presentation of the deity, it is possible to investigate common themes running through several works. This chapter will follow that approach and will examine the use of imagery drawn from human family life to describe the relationship between God and his people. Key images are those of God the father and the husband. The first of these topics is illustrated by the following prophetic text:

For you, O Lord, are our father; our Redeemer from of old is your name. (Isa 63:16).

What should the reader make of the above quotation? The Christian tradition has made of this type of language its focal image of God. Following the model of Jesus at prayer presented in the Synoptic Gospels (Matthew, Mark, Luke) as someone who calls upon 'God, My Father',[1] Christian writers have identified the deity as a father figure. God is father to Jesus of Nazareth in a special sense, since the Gospel of John, for instance, describes Jesus as God's 'only-begotten Son'.[2] But, since Jesus calls all those who follow him brothers and sisters, God is also to be viewed as 'Our Father'.[3] This use of language opens up several issues, such as 'In what way can God be a father to human beings?' and 'What are the contemporary religious and cultural consequences of stressing the relationship of a father to a son as means of access to a universal deity?'

God is both like and unlike a human parent. First it has to be stated that there is an inevitable gap — the Lord of Israel does not have sexual relations with a feminine being and so produce children — unlike the gods of other ancient Near Eastern religions.[4] However God, whether as Elohim or YHWH, is described as a single male; that is, the masculine singular form of verbs is used with the divine name. It follows from this grammatical fact that the pronoun 'he' may be properly used for the deity.

The intimacy of the link between human parenthood and divine paternity is balanced, in the OT, against images of transcendence; God is infinitely superior to human beings. Both the Flood story in Genesis 6 – 9 and the scene in Job where God appears in the whirlwind (ch. 38) point to the existential gap which lies between God and human beings. In the first of these texts God stands in judgement on human acts, and in the second the deity's rhetorical questions are designed to highlight the inferiority of human wisdom to that of God. In this context God can be more suitably defined as 'non-human', a 'spiritual' rather than a 'physical' being.

But can human beings find daily contact with a remote divine existence? The OT images of God freely use human images familiar to the reader to bring the deity close: as with images such as shepherd, king, warrior ... All of these terms would enable a reader in the ancient world to understand more of the nature of YHWH. It is within this setting that the image of the fatherhood of God can be viewed as meaningful. For YHWH is a single male deity with no divine partner and no family of named children in the OT[5] — a reality which makes it possible for human beings to fill the vacuum left by the absence of a pantheon of gods, the divine family. Whereas Mesopotamian religion views human beings as mere slaves of the gods,[6] human beings in the OT are servants of God of some nobility and standing. The Lord of Israel is portrayed as taking great pains with these created beings who, in Genesis 1 are given a place of dominion in the universe.

The fatherhood of God thus serves to give a positive and optimistic setting for human existence, that of good parental nurture. All that is necessary can be asked of God in prayer, as one modern Christian hymn reminds the reader.[7] The key emotion attached to this image of God is love — not the covenantal loyalty of *hesed* so much as the intimate bond between two human lovers (*ahab*). A study by J. Miles aptly summarizes this development of religious thought.[8] In his treatment of the book of Isaiah, Miles points out the movement of thought from God as a judge saddened by the need to pass sentence on sinful beings to God as a husband seeking out the forsaken wife and bringing her joy through his compassionate treatment of her: 'He discovers, for the first time, what it means to love her. He discovers that he had never truly loved her before. He takes her back ....'[9]

This God of love finds expression in prophecy in the theme of a loving father and husband who finds his care unreciprocated by offspring and partner. Thus Isaiah 63 talks of Israel as God's children and of God as 'our father'. In verse 16 it is precisely as father that God acts as redeemer of the nation, treating them as a family branch in need of tender care. The next chapter also calls on God to intervene because he is father, giving identity to his offspring just as a potter gives shape to clay (Isa 64:8). In this context of the paternity of God human beings are viewed as children of the divine family. They are described by prophets as 'rebellious children', as in Isaiah 30. But they are also cherished sons, as can be seen from Hosea 11:1:

When Israel was a child I loved him, and out of Egypt I called my son ...

This language of father and children stresses the intimacy of the relationship between Israel and its Lord. Despite the disaster of invasion and deportation, God will not abandon Israel and Judah. As a loving parent cannot abandon offspring, so God can be relied upon to renew the fortunes of the nation. This image is one of security and is intended to be reassuring for human readers. But is that the whole story? Deeper examination of the issues involved raises doubts about the contemporary value of imaging God as father.

In the late twentieth century some queries have been raised about the helpfulness of this image of the deity as father. Recent social surveys in European countries have indicated that children do not always learn of outpouring nurture from their actual parents. God as a father may raise up thoughts of a distant and even oppressive figure. Y. Spiegel, for example, wrote in the 1980s,[10] about a fatherly god not characterized by love, 'God becomes the silent father, who is absent though present, who cannot be appealed to and withdraws from questions as well as from requests...'.[11]

There is a further objection which can be raised here. So far it has been shown that the image is of God as father and Israel as sons. This puts the stress on the masculine in the relationship of God and people. Is God, then, a male figure in essence? Are only sons valuable to this deity? What about daughters? It is possible to redress the balance somewhat, since the texts of prophecy do indeed contain feminine references.

God himself is addressed in terms reminiscent of mother as well as father. Thus the image of God as a divine warrior, brandishing his weapons in battle, in Isaiah 42:13 leads immediately to the image of God in labour, crying out in childbirth:

now I will cry out like a woman in labour, I will gasp and pant. (v. 14)

The tenderness of maternal care and its power for nurture becomes an image for divine protection in Isaiah 66:12–13:

... you shall nurse and be carried on her arm, and dandled on her knees. As a mother comforts her child, so I will comfort you; ...

At the same time the nation is addressed not only as sons but as daughters. Isaiah 37:22 calls Jerusalem 'virgin daughter Zion ...' and Jeremiah 31:21 addresses 'virgin Israel'. However, this imagery is often used in a negative context. Thus in the Isaianic passage cited above, the message concerns the arrogant defiance of God on the daughter's part and in the Jeremianic passage virgin Israel is defined as 'faithless daughter'. The image of a defiled and humiliated woman is frequently found in the texts which deal with Israel's sin and punishment from God. Amos 5:2, for instance, describes the invasion of Israel like this:

Fallen, no more to rise, is maiden Israel; forsaken on her land, with no one to raise her up.

It is not just the results of failing to keep God's laws which are illustrated by this language style. The sinning itself is described in the language code of 'fallen women' whose free use of sexual powers has brought dishonour and shame. Isaiah 1:21, for example, attacks Jerusalem in this way:

How the faithful city has become a whore! She that was full of justice, righteousness lodged in her — but now murderers!

The version of this theme to be found in Ezekiel is extreme in its dwelling on the details of female sexual activity as a model for the people of Samaria and Judah having worshipped gods other than YHWH.[12]

It can be argued, then, that imaging God as father has some drawbacks, both in terms of the father image itself and in terms of stressing masculinity in the deity. The comment that, in fact, in prophecy God is also a mother and Israel is not only son but also daughter, can be met by the response that son can be a positive as well as a negative image for the nation whereas daughter is more often negative.

The second image of God which takes its meaning from family life is that of God the husband. This image, too, has the potential for reassuring the reader concerning the intimacy of the deity with his people, since it envisages the secure image of faithful partners in mutual support of one another. Hosea 1 − 2 is the classic text here. God is a good husband who remains faithful and constantly desires the proper renewal of relationship with his wife, Israel. Even though prophet and deity for a time divorce their partners, this separation is overturned and a new marriage contract is drawn up (Hos 2). Longer prophetic books make use of the same metaphor. Thus Jeremiah images God as the faithful divine husband of Israel who is offended by his wife's (the nation's) behaviour. Chapter 2 explores this charge, as does chapter 3. As with Hosea so here also the later part of the book uses the image of bride replacing that of whore for a picture of divine salvation. The renewal of marriage makes the nation like a young woman ready for marriage to a loving husband (Jer 31:3–5, for instance).

But to what sort of readers does all this language appeal? Modern commentators, especially female ones, have pointed out that this use of female imagery is for the benefit of men. True worshippers of the Lord are like good husbands and fathers, false ones are like common whores. The feminine is the metaphor for all that is bad and deceitful in this context. This tendency within the literature is the result of its being written within a paternalistic culture, called by feminist writers 'patriarchy'. In such a culture women are daughters and wives, the property of fathers and husbands. The area of sexual activity is of great significance here. A daughter's value is her virginity which gives her father the bride price. A wife's value is her availability for sexual attention from her husband and from no other. Women who break out of these social boundaries and use their sexual powers for their personal interest bring on their families only shame and disgrace. It is these social realities which have become, in the OT, the bases for the images of God as father and husband.

Women readers of the OT have reacted variously to this image of God as husband and its companion image, woman as sinful. Although many modern women cannot simply accept this image of God as valuable, as it stands, some have abandoned the OT images of God completely whereas others have attempted to find the more positively feminine messages hidden within the patriarchal text. This is an area of biblical exegesis which has attracted enormous interest in recent years; a selection of feminine thoughts will be examined here, but what follows is a selection rather than a comprehensive survey.

In a study published in 1981,[13] R. Radford Ruether outlined what have become the 'classical' problems of the use of male images for the deity. Her essay begins by asserting that 'the exclusively male image of God in the Judaeo-Christian tradition has become a critical issue of contemporary religious life'.[14]

This male imaging of God is an ideological bias that reflects the sociology of patriarchal societies, societies dominated by a male, property-owning head of household. God is such a male householder in prophetic books which use father imagery for the deity. In the OT there is only one deity, a male, a focus of interest for other fathers and husbands, but not a figure which directly addresses women as equals. This use of male imagery reinforces the social teaching that women are of less value in society than men. The overall effect of this social context of language is that the image of a male God as father and husband serves to subordinate women:

The 'feminine' in patriarchal society is basically allowed to act only within the same, limited, subordinate or mediating roles that women are allowed to act in the patriarchal social order. The feminine is the recipient and mediator of male power to subordinate persons ... [15]

Reuther's response, in this essay, is to move from the Judaeo-Christian tradition towards a religion which draws on the ancient goddess figure found in many religions:

A God(dess) who is a good parent, and not a neurotic parent, is one that promotes our growth towards responsible personhood, not one who sanctions dependency.[16]

Ruether thus outlines the broad theological issues connected with male images of God. A. Laffey's book *Wives, Harlots and Concubines*[17] explores the roles of women in the OT. Having defined the term 'patriarchy' and its relevance for the study of the OT,[18] Laffey argues that the result of discovering patriarchal bias in the texts may be despair of ever finding anything helpful in the collection.[19] However, it is possible to find feminine images and messages hidden within the text, hidden because they do not form the direct focus of the author but have almost got into the text by accident. Such are the nameless women referred to in many passages as wives, harlots or concubines to OT men.

When she turns to prophetic imagery, Laffey points out that the main vocabulary of these texts relates to national history, history which is male-centred since its main protagonists — God, king, prophet — are all male figures. However there are, for instance, descriptions of cities as female figures, even though these may be negative as well as positive metaphors:

The prophetic writings describe punishment — sometimes for Israel, sometimes for Judah, sometimes for their enemies — with female imagery. They use symbols which portray women being deprived of their identity and their destiny as wives and mothers ... The prophetic writings also describe Judah's restoration with female imagery... [20]

This imagery is derived, as has been argued above, from male-centred imagery of God as father and husband. However, it can be of interest for women readers and does give some role to the female in relation to divine activity. One aspect of this is that women can stand as images for all powerless and marginalized persons in society. Since the prophetic books generally convey a concern for the rights of the poor and powerless in relation to greedy, powerful leaders of society, this gives dignity even to a 'weak' image of woman.

Laffey picks out passages in prophetic texts which invite the opinion of women readers. These range from texts which use negative images of woman to balance positive images of men, woman as God's adulterous wife, for example, to passages where women are given authority and power. Hosea 1 – 2 describes divine compassion in female images of the womb-derived love which a mother has. Jeremiah 31:22 describes a 'new thing' on earth: a woman 'protects a man'. Here the redeemer role of the deity acquires a female aspect. Laffey's concluding remarks on prophetic imagery highlights the tension caused between reader and text by images of God as father and husband. Specific to prophetic literature is the metaphor of a woman to signify a country, city or people which is in relationship with the deity. Also in a positive vein is the fact that women's experiences, such as anguish at childbirth, nurturing and rearing, are employed as images of the divine. But these usages are in tension with, and may well be outweighed by, the presentation of woman as the type of offence against the deity. Faithless women are the lowest of the low in patriarchal society:

To portray Yahweh as male while portraying faithless Israel and faithless Judah as females was unjustly to relegate the female sex to an inferior status from which it has not yet recovered.[21]

P. Trible's study of *God and the Rhetoric of Sexuality* also addresses male imagery for the deity from an OT perspective.[22] Trible picks up on the description of human beings as made in the divine image in Genesis 1:27. She works with this metaphor to raise the possibility of appropriately describing God through the language of human sexuality. *Ha-adam* (man) in the verse from Genesis refers to humankind, Trible argues, rather than to a male human being. From humankind emerges two complementary aspects, that of male and female. Thus imaging the divine involves both men and women equally.[23] It is an extension of this use of metaphorical language to discuss God through the concept of maternal womb imagery, a subject to which Trible now turns. She states:

Associations of God with the uterus expand in the poetic literature of Israel. Not only does Yahweh control fertility by closing and opening the womb, but also this deity works in the organ itself to mould individual life....[24]

Linked to this divine control of human fertility is the image of God as merciful. 'Yahweh merciful and gracious belongs to recitals of the saving acts of God in history.'[25] The term *raham* in Hebrew refers to an emotion which stems from the inner parts — the womb is, then, a natural translation for this concept. 'Thus an exclusively female image extends its meaning to a divine mode of being. "I will truly show motherly-compassion upon him," says Yahweh.'[26] Trible's work allows the reader to approach prophetic descriptions of God through positive, female images. Hosea, Jeremiah and second Isaiah all use this language of divine compassion. For instance, in Isaiah 49:15 YHWH asks whether a mother can forget her baby and states that it can happen, but (s)he will never forget the nation. Trible concludes this chapter with the view that:

with persistence and power the root RHM journeys throughout the traditions of Israel to establish a major metaphor for biblical faith: semantic movement from the wombs of women to the compassion of God.[27]

In this study Trible is an example of a woman reader who can find new ways to adapt and so to adopt, the prophetic language of God as parent.

Her comments show Trible to be a woman disposed to find God (man) / People (woman) imagery helpful in bringing the reader to a deeper understanding of divine care, as opposed to Ruether, for example, who turns to a more centrally feminine image of the god(dess). Another book which also talks of finding constructive feminine images in the OT is that of J. W. H. van Wijk-Bos.[28] Wijk-Bos points out, in her introduction, that the topic of women and God now arouses a great deal of interest among popular audiences. It is this current concern which leads her to re-imagine God.

In her initial chapters Wijk-Bos discusses the foundations for helpful debate about God. She refers to E. Johnson's work and to Johnson's question about the right way to speak of God '... in the face of women's newly cherished human dignity and equality'. The context for this enterprise is patriarchy, which

creates an organization of structures with men in charge ... Feminist theologians view patriarchy ... as a sin, in agreement with Elizabeth Johnson's statement that 'sexism is a sin ...'.[29]

In line with this approach, Wijk-Bos wishes to establish a neutral gender base for the reader's first contact with the OT god. This base can be found in the ambiguity of the several names and titles of God in the OT. Elohim is neutral since it comes to denote a universal deity whose transcendence puts God beyond gender. El Shaddai has often been translated as 'Almighty God', as if connected with the term for high mountains. This is at least neutral but can even be read as more positively feminine, since the meaning of Shaddai has always been difficult to pin down; it could equally well derive from the term for breasts, *shaddayim* in Hebrew.[30] YHWH as a divine name has to do with existence, but this is a category broader than a male or female life. It does indeed have 'universal' possibilities. Ultimately, as Holy One, God is both present to Israel and yet other than human:

While the holiness of God points to God's otherness, it also lays claim on the human community in whose midst God is present as the Holy One. God's holiness issues a call to the community that names God holy, to mirror God's justice and righteousness.[31]

In the later part of her study Wijk-Bos applies this manner of approaching God to the debate about the feminine and the deity. This brings her to the prophetic images of God as parent. Wijk-Bos discusses the image of God as woman in childbirth as well as the image of God as a mother protesting her faithful love of her infant.[32] In the image of divine comforter 'God as comforting mother takes the place of mother Jerusalem'.[33] From this survey the writer concludes that maternal imagery is a broad topic in the OT, especially if other related terms are included such as 'womb-compassion'. She states:

It is important to become aware of such possible references, for it would be unfortunate if we remain locked into overwhelmingly male imagery for God with some 'added' maternal characteristics.[34]

Whereas Wijk-Bos highlights the possibility of imaging God from the OT as parent rather than father, by including images of both parents, male and female, and so retrieves the value for readers of this traditional image of God, C. J. Exum's book[35] contains a chapter which thoroughly condemns the other parallel image, that of God the husband. In her chapter entitled 'Prophetic pornography', Exum touches upon the images used for sinful Israel in prophetic books: 'These texts contain shocking and scandalising language. Not surprisingly, most translations tone them down ...'[36]

   In these images men use fantasies about female powers of sexuality as descriptions of total separation from God. In passages in the three major works of prophecy male authors dwell on female sexuality:

The female gaze is postulated in order to be condemned, while readers are invited to assume the text's male gaze at the women's genitalia. The intrusive textual gaze remains fixed upon the female body and its humiliation in the following verses, where images are resolved in a picture of Zion as a ravaged woman.[37]

Ezekiel, in particular, provides an example of this form of imagery. And the most extreme example of the book is in chapter 23 where the two sisters, Oholah and Oholibah, serve as metaphors for the two kingdoms of Samaria and Judah. Exum comments on the movement of the text: the prophet seems to take pleasure in detailing the sexual activity of each sister before going on to describe the abusive fate which awaits them at male hands. 'One of God's wives, the northern kingdom, dies as a result of abuse. God threatens his other wife with the same treatment.'[38]

   In these scenes, Exum claims, God participates in biblical violence where physical abuse is the divine method of re-asserting control over the women.

   The problem here is not just the violence, but the ideology which lies behind it. Harlotry only has meaning in relation to women's bodies and can apply to males only metaphorically:

This ideology gives rise to the prophetic marriage metaphor in which the unquestioned superior male position is further privileged by placing God in the husband's position.[39]

In this setting God is a person who connives at male ill-treatment of women, who takes delight in the physical stripping, rape and killing of females. Claiming that behind all this imagery there is in fact a kind and caring person will not make the problem go away, Exum argues. The long-term effect is immense since the reader is drawn to take biblical texts as role models for religious and social behaviour. What can be done? Exum turns to some recent women's commentaries on the cultural influences of the OT to suggest some starting-points.

One important task for women readers is to read against the grain of the text. Prophetic violence texts require women to see themselves as in the wrong, as proper targets for male violence. The task of commentators is, then, to name the issues at stake for women and to resist the rhetorical persuasiveness of the text being read. From this comes the possibility of denying meaning to this image of God as in any way helpful to the mature development of either women or men readers of the OT. Exum continues:

And, I would add, I think it important to recognise that God is a character in the biblical narrative (as much a male construct as the women in biblical literature) and thus not to be confused with any one's notion of a 'real' god.[40]

Exum thus not only criticizes the image of God as husband in the manner in which it is utilized by Israelite prophecy, she also throws doubt on the sanctity of the image itself. Whereas other writers may try to retrieve traditional images by bringing to the reader's attention some positive elements which they may not have noticed — God as mother as well as father, for instance, or the reversal of divorce and shame as husband takes back the wife of his youth — Exum makes no such attempt to restore the prophetic use of male and female imagery to pride of place. The image is simply that, an image of the deity shaped and moulded by human attitudes and social values. God is set free from this image, God exists outside of it. Humans will have to seek God anew and develop fresh and more appropriate imaging to convey the meaning of a universal divine being.

Among these feminist studies of the image of God as father and husband there is a great range of opinion, with two opposing tendencies at base — that of trying to find a way of remaining sympathetic to the deity portrayed by the OT and that of a radical separation from that figure. Whichever position is taken up by the readers of the present book, the underlying issues remain alive and active in modern society. The Christian tradition has long rooted itself in biblical imagery and this has continuing effects on Christian social organization and attitudes. A number of women commentators[41] on the prejudice against women expressed in communities which base themselves on biblical imagery point out that this is a matter which concerns not just women but all marginalized and oppressed members of society. Whilst prophetic texts which convey the image of God as father and husband have traditionally been interpreted as texts of hope since they reveal the long-suffering patience of God, for many modern women readers they can appear as texts of terror which endorse the continuing use of social violence against 'lower-class citizens' — a title long given to the female members of society.

Summary

This chapter focuses on the manner in which the OT regards God as forming a family unit with human beings, with his people Israel. The images of God as father and husband have been presented as a source of comfort in the past but they are now viewed as controversial, since they imply the high value of maleness as opposed to the secondary social status of females. There is a great deal of current writing on this area of images of God and the present chapter can only survey some of the field, pointing out the varying tendencies of feminist critique.

Notes

1 This is a translation of the Aramaic *Abba*. It is a word which typifies Jesus' prayer attitude to God. Contrary to older interpretations of this as equivalent to 'Daddy' (J. Jeremias), G. Vermes has pointed out that it would be more appropriate, in the context of first-century Judaism, to translate it as a reverential but intimate invocation, 'My father'.

2 As in John 1:18, where the point of the Son as only-begotten is to stress the close link between the deity and Jesus, to identify Jesus as indeed himself divine.

3 As in the Lord's Prayer in Matthew 6:9–13 and Luke 11:2–4.

4 It is a general truth that the myths and legends of ancient Near Eastern religions refer to a number of deities related to one another as in a human family. See, for instance, the stories of the Graeco-Roman pantheon or the text of Ugaritic Baal legends.

5 It is correct to say that there is no clear divine family in the OT. There are, however, some unclear references to 'sons of God' as in Genesis 6 and Job 1. Generally these are taken to be references to angels, rather than to actual deities, but there are polytheistic echoes in this language.

6 See, for instance, the Mesopotamian story of Atrahasis in J. B. Pritchard (ed.), *Ancient Near Eastern Texts Relating to the Old Testament* (Princeton: Princeton University Press, 1969).

7 The words of this evangelical chorus written by J. M. Scriven are, in fact, 'Have you trials or tribulations ... take them to the Lord in prayer ...'. See I. Bradley (ed.) *The Penguin Book of Hymns* (London: Viking, 1989).

8 Cf. J. Miles, *God: A Biography* (New York: Simon & Schuster, 1995).

9 Miles (1995), p. 243.

10 Y. Spiegel, 'God the father in the fatherless society' in J. Metz and E. Schillebeeckx (eds), *God As Father, Concilium* 143 (Edinburgh: T. & T. Clark, 1981).

11 Spiegel (1981), p. 6.

12 See here chapters 16 and 23 of the book of Ezekiel. Although they are sacred texts for Jews and Christians they might otherwise be classed as pornographic in intent.

13 R. Radford Ruether, 'The female nature of God: a problem in contemporary religious life' in Metz and Schillebeeckx (eds) (1981).
14 Ruether (1981), p. 61.
15 Ruether (1981), p. 64.
16 Ruether (1981), p. 65.
17 A. L. Laffey, *Wives, Harlots and Concubines* (Philadelphia: Fortress, 1988).
18 Laffey (1988), p. 2.
19 Laffey (1988), p. 3.
20 Laffey (1988), p. 164.
21 Laffey (1988), p. 178.
22 P. Trible, *God and the Rhetoric of Sexuality* (London: SCM Press, 1978).
23 Trible (1978), p. 18.
24 Trible (1978), p. 35.
25 Trible (1978), p. 39.
26 Trible (1978), p. 45.
27 Trible (1978), p. 56.
28 J. W. H. van Wijk-Bos, *Re-imagining God: The Case for Scriptural Diversity* (Louisville: John Knox, 1995).
29 Wijk-Bos (1995), p. 3.
30 Wijk-Bos (1995), pp. 26–8.
31 Wijk-Bos (1995), p. 33.
32 Wijk-Bos (1995), pp. 51–62.
33 Wijk-Bos (1995), p. 63.
34 Wijk-Bos (1995), p. 65.
35 J. Cheryl Exum, *Plotted, Shot and Painted: Cultural Representations of Biblical Women* (Sheffield: Sheffield Academic Press, 1996).
36 Exum (1996), p. 103.
37 Exum (1996), p. 106.
38 Exum (1996), p. 109.
39 Exum (1996), p. 113.
40 Exum (1996), p. 112.
41 See, for instance, J. Chittister, *WomanStrength* (London: Sheed & Ward, 1990); chapter 1 of this book treats the issue of long-term discrimination against women in Christian circles.

8 God and the Temple in Ezekiel

This third chapter on images of God in prophecy returns to a focus on one single work, that of the book of Ezekiel. This text is counted among the major prophetic books of the OT and is presented as the writings of a priest from Judah while he was in exile in Babylon in the sixth century BCE.[1] Not surprisingly, perhaps, the book focuses on images of God connected with the symbols of worship used in the Jerusalem Temple. The central reference here is to the Glory of God, a term which refers to the throne-chariot of God seen by the exiled prophet in a series of visions.

There are a number of similarities between this text and that of the other two major works of prophecy, Isaiah and Jeremiah. All three texts contain similar material — judgement oracles against Judah / Israel, judgement oracles against the nations, and salvation oracles for Jerusalem and Judah. Ezekiel, however, is ultimately a singular work. Compared with the other two major works, it contains much more prose material then they do and much less poetry, a trait marked in the oracles themselves. In Ezekiel these are delivered generally in prose as opposed to the more usual poetic oracle forms of other prophetic books.

In addition, there are a number of signature phrases used by the prophet. These include the manner of divine address to the prophet, namely 'Son of Man' and the consistent designation of the sins of the people as offences against the purity and holiness of the deity. More than any other major work of written prophecy, Ezekiel offers evidence of the role of divine inspiration as the source and support of the work of a prophet. This creates a link with the careers of Elijah and Elisha as delineated in the books of Kings. Within this spirit-filled environment a number of unusual events take place. Ezekiel is lifted up in the spirit and transported across the land (Ezek 3:14). He is asked to perform strange actions such as swallowing a scroll (Ezek 3:1–3), and lying on his side for 390 days without moving (Ezek 4). This type of activity, connected with the theme of the prophet's loss of speech (Ezek 3:26), and allied to the extremely sexual language used in some of the judgement speeches of the prophet (Ezek 16 and 23), has led to the bestowal of the adjective 'bizarre' on this prophetic work.[2]

It is certainly the case that the text appears strange to a modern reader. But this may be due to the gap between contemporary European theological language and concepts and those of the ancient Near East — a topic which has already been addressed in the chapter on law and covenant. In order to understand the overall coherence of the religious world evidenced by the book of Ezekiel, it will be necessary to investigate in greater depth the conceptual framework of Temple and worship, a theme which has been addressed by recent scholarship.

The theme of Temple permeates the entire thought-world of the prophet Ezekiel. The introduction to the prophet's work focuses on a vision of the presence of the Lord of Israel, described in the imagery of the *merkabah* or throne-chariot. This vision should probably be connected with the Ark of the Lord referred to in the Deuteronomistic history as the cultic object which symbolized the presence of the Lord. As such it was carried into battle and brought victory to the nation.[3] T. Longman and D. Reid give an account of the military setting of the Ark in their book, *God Is a Warrior*.[4] The description of the Ark is confusing, since some texts refer to it as though it were a chest in which sacred objects could be placed (Exod 25). In the Psalms, however, it appears to be rather more than this since God can be seated on it and it is surrounded by supernatural guardian spirits, the cherubim. It is this second version of the Ark of the Lord which can be situated in a Temple context. In 2 Samuel David brings the Ark to reside in Jerusalem; in 1 Kings Solomon constructs a Temple which houses the Ark.

The priestly setting of Ezekiel provides a link with the Ark as a sign of the sacred presence; it is Ark as throne-chariot which is the central image here. The throne-chariot continues to be the key symbol for the divine presence in the book of Ezekiel. Described as the Glory of God, it initiates the prophet's work at the start of the book and is the source of his inspiration. The Glory of God is to be seen in Jerusalem, passing judgement on the city, in the earlier chapters of the book.[5] The final judgement of God on the city and divine abandonment of the people is symbolized by the lifting up of the chariot and its flight away from the Temple:

Then the cherubim lifted up their wings, with the wheels beside them; and the glory of the God of Israel was above them. And the glory of the Lord ascended from the middle of the city, and stopped on the mountain east of the city. (Ezek 11:22–23)

In the final sections of the text the Glory of God returns to a future, restored Temple and once again makes a home for itself within Judah and Jerusalem:

As the glory of the Lord entered the temple by the gate facing east, the spirit lifted me up, and brought me into the inner court; and the glory of the Lord filled the temple. (Ezek 43:4–5)

The work of the prophet is linked to the theme of the Ark since it is a voice from the chariot which commands the prophet to speak and act as a messenger of God. As such a messenger, Ezekiel is placed among the host of supernatural servants of the deity. He is led into visionary experience by the sight of heavenly beings who mediate the divine to him. The vision of the Temple restoration, for instance, is mediated by a man

whose appearance shone like bronze, with a linen cord and a measuring reed in his hand (Ezek 40:3)

while earlier visions involved a figure

that looked like a human being; below what appeared to be its loins it was fire, and above the loins it was like the appearance of brightness ... It stretched out the form of a hand, and took me by a lock of my head ... (Ezek 8:2–3)

In this context the prophet himself is titled Son of Man, thus symbolically entering the heavenly army of God's servants. A further depth of meaning for this title can be found by comparing Ezekiel with the non-canonical Jewish work, the book of *Enoch*. In the account of Jewish history given in that work, in an animal fable, characters which appear as angels of God in the OT are defined by the phrase 'One like a Son of Man'.[6] All that Ezekiel says and does, then, has to be viewed not from the human field of everyday life experience, but from the perspective of overarching divine reality. He becomes another source of mediation of divine truth to the human situation, transformed by the divine spirit into a messenger of the Divine Assembly.

Further evidence of the cultic background of the book of Ezekiel is to be found in the nature of the prophet's message. The prophet passes on God's judgement against the people who are guilty of sinning against their god and so deserving of divine punishment. This message Ezekiel shares with the other prophets, but the focus of prophetic condemnation is somewhat different. Whereas Isaiah, for instance, looks to social injustice as well as false religion as the cause of Judah's downfall, Ezekiel features largely the religious failures of Jerusalem. The Jerusalem Temple signifies the whole population which is judged. It is the false religion carried on in the sanctuary which causes offence, as in Ezekiel 8. Here the prophet is brought by a heavenly being to the Temple court and told to dig a hole by which to enter in. He is then directed to go in and see the vile abominations which are taking place inside the cult centre:

... there, portrayed on the wall all around, were all kinds of creeping things, and loathsome animals, and all the idols of the house of Israel. Before them stood seventy of the elders of the house of Israel ... Each had his censer in his hand, and the fragrant cloud of incense was ascending. (Ezek 8:10–11)

Chapter 7, which offers a general oracle of judgement on the people, nonetheless illustrates the root of national offence as false cultic activity:

Their silver and gold cannot save them ... For it was the stumbling block of their iniquity. From their beautiful ornament ... they made their abominable images, their detestable things; therefore I will make of it an unclean thing to them. (Ezek 7:19–20)

In all these ways Ezekiel is a book which lives and breathes cultic imagery and cultic language. God is pre-eminently holy, separated from the people because they have abandoned holiness and turned to impurity. The sinfulness of the people is commonly described by the terms 'abominations' and 'detestable things'. This language also is rooted in a priestly world-view. There are resonances here between the language of Ezekiel and that of Leviticus. From a cultic perspective the supremacy of the deity can be expressed by the image of purity. That which is holy is pure. To safeguard divine supremacy there must be no informal contact between what is pure and what is impure; there can be no mixing of species. The realm of God is purity and that purity resides in the Holy of Holies in the Temple. For a human to enter the purity of God he must first be separated out from the everyday world and set aside formally for his new role. He must wear special clothing and be prepared by washing and by abstaining from human activity of eating and sexual intimacy. These are some of the ground rules for creating priests to mediate between God and society which are to be found in Leviticus.[7] Furthermore, all Israelites must maintain ritual purity in order to offer legitimate sacrifice to God by joining in Temple worship. The theme of holiness underpins the second part of Leviticus where the conditions which cause impurity are outlined together with the means of cleansing from impurity before the Lord of Israel.

Ezekiel shares this code of language. The sin of the people is viewed as ritual defilement which makes their worship itself impure. The very Temple is defiled so badly that the Glory of God must abandon it. However, God intends to create a new sanctuary for Israel to gather around, once the old has been cleansed of impurity. The foreign invasions here turn into a form of heavenly cleansing of an impure city and also of an impure people with whom God can no longer reside. Thus, in chapter 10, the prophet sees burning coals taken from the heavenly sanctuary, from under the wheels of the throne-chariot, and scattered over the city.

It is to be noted that the Lord of Israel is the mover of events in this sequence, rather than the people of the city. Ezekiel envisages a state of affairs in which the people are inherently incapable of turning away from defilement. In chapter 20 of the book the Lord speaks to the nation about their past history, pointing out that the nation has, in each age, been sinful and turned away from its Lord. Just as the ransomed slaves turned against God in the wilderness and were faced with divine judgement, so now a further generation has turned against God in the land. God will bring them into the wilderness of exile and once again the nation will face the wrath of its deity. But all this is not so much to teach the people about their own nature as to teach the nations about the nature of the Lord of Israel. P. M. Joyce, in his study of divine initiative in Ezekiel,[8] points out the focus of the text on the divine name. Again and again the Lord of Israel announces that he will punish his people so that they may know that 'I am Yahweh'. Joyce states that 'our formula [I am YHWH] has, then, a broad range of application, Yahweh revealing his essential nature in both judgement and deliverance'.[9] God will defend the holiness of his name and require worship on his holy mountain (Ezek 20:40). He will bring the people back so that they may perform this cult for the Lord of Israel; but all of this is to ensure that the holiness and purity of God remained unsullied, that his repute is undamaged:

And you shall know that I am the Lord, when I deal with you for my name's sake, not according to your evil ways ... O house of Israel, says the Lord God. (Ezek 20:44)

God is here presented as absolutely other, powerfully transcendent. There is no human claim which can be made on this deity but mercy will come to human beings because that is part of God's own identity, the witness to his holiness. As P. M. Joyce argues,

the ultimate motive of Yahweh's activity is found in his desire to vindicate his 'name', the primary content of which is, it seems, not his reputation as a compassionate, forgiving or even a just god, but rather his reputation as a powerful deity.[10]

'Holiness' and 'defilement' are a pair of terms which can define the health of a given society as well as defining the nature of God. They form a complete world-view within which individual actions can be measured. Thus they provide for a system of social structure in which morality is measured by the concept of contagion. Purity and impurity are caught, transmitted from person to person, from object to person, from person to object. It is this ideological framework, described by commentators on the OT as 'priestly', which underlies the prophet's critique of Jerusalem society in the sixth century BCE. At one end of the scale the deity is totally holy, at the other end the people are totally defiled and the source of spreading corruption. The book of Leviticus is a text which fills in the background of holiness, since its message is entirely shaped by the poles of purity and impurity.

A recent study of Leviticus has examined aspects of the text's thought-world.[11] The initial chapters of this study justify the task of reading the book as a single, coherent text rather than as a series of law codes embedded in the larger sequence of text from Exodus to Numbers. Granted this approach, it is then possible to examine particular aspects of the book's message. J. Milgrom's article[12] reflects on the nature of holiness as a concept within Leviticus. He balances the two parts of the book against each other to arrive at a final meaning. The first chapters (designated as P [for priestly]) have a rigid concept of holiness in which God alone is holy. This holiness can be extended to priests in a formal manner in order that the deity can be offered worship. Thus there is sacred space and time, that is, a sanctuary and festivals,[13] together with human beings to operate within that designated holy space and time. The later chapters of the book (designated as H [for holy]) loosen the rigidity of P. Chapter 19 marks a new stage of thought since it announces to the reader 'You shall be holy, for I the Lord your God am holy'.[14] Thus holiness is extended in H to the whole land and the whole people. Milgrom regards this as the author's answer to prophetic attacks on land and people as unholy, as sinful and impure. The book announces a code for enabling human life experience to be cleansed of defilement and to be acceptable to God:

In chapter 19, H brims with hope that all Israel will heed the divine call to holiness, and hence there is no reason to anticipate a purge of the nation.[15]

The chapter contributed by M. Douglas[16] adds a further dimension to the concept of holiness. Douglas takes as her foundation the view that religious concepts cannot be examined as intellectual matters but must be situated in the lives and experiences of believers.[17] In this context the laws concerning ritual purity and holiness should be seen not as requirements made by a vindictive deity who seeks to oppress further those already troubled by physical distress, but rather as a method by which a society controls blame and punishment. The basis of this system is the term 'contagion'. Sacred contagion concerns the way in which sin is spread in a society: 'Under the prophets and judges it was unpredictable, only a prophet could say where it was going to strike next ...'[18]

By contrast, Leviticus bureaucratizes sin and so both expands and limits its scope. All human beings are now liable to defilement,[19] but there are also limits to blame. Someone with a skin disease should be put out of the group while the disease lasts but can be re-admitted after it has faded. Men and women will be made unclean through emissions of fluid connected with their sexuality, but the length of time involved in defilement is fixed and limited. The consequence of this construct of holiness and defilement is the establishment of a stable social system which prevents the unpredictable victimization of individuals and abuse of social power.[20] Furthermore;

The people of Israel have only to repent, and the Lord will forgive. He has given them the means to reach him and to make reparation for their transgressions.[21]

The arguments of Milgrom and Douglas offer the reader new horizons on the OT ideology of holiness. Their research suggests that the theme of holiness is not peripheral to OT ideas about God and the world, but is at the centre of the relationship between them. This entails viewing holiness as a positive idea, as something which aids human ideals of fairness and equality and not as rigid or negative. This brings back to mind the chapter on law and covenant, earlier in this book, where it was noted that the OT is more likely to regard freedom and security for human beings as a product of order and stability than of a barely controlled free-for-all conflict between competing interests. Ezekiel, by focusing on the prevalence of defilement in Israelite society, endorses the high value of purity which is now maintained solely within the divine sphere of activity. Holiness is what human society needs but cannot attain by its own efforts.

The broader setting of the debate about holiness in Ezekiel is the presence of God in the Jerusalem Temple. The prophet's visions of the Glory of God and its actions take their meaning from the nature of cult and its ideological framework. Recent scholarship has made these matters more accessible to the contemporary reader of the OT. Contrary to earlier scholarly opinion which claimed that the OT did not have a mythological base, writers such as M. Barker and R. Murray have suggested that the present OT collection does, indeed, show traces of a mythology which undergirded religious practice at central worship sites in Israel / Judah.

M. Barker has made a study of the Jerusalem Temple and the influence of its ideology in the Bible and in first-century Jewish texts.[22] She begins by rehearsing the evidence for the construction of the Temple and the development of its cultic activities. Central to the daily round of events in the Temple was the offering of sacrifice, often consisting of animal sacrifice on the great altar. Days and years took their meaning from the sacred calendar which laid down a pattern of seasonal feasts, marked by the movement of the sun and moon through the heavens.[23]

Granted the existence of a sacred site with a developed life of its own, what can be said about the deeper meaning of such a cult centre? Barker turns to the theme of 'garden' for an explanation.[24] Drawing on many sources both within the Bible and in non-canonical Jewish and Christian works, Barker points out that gods were generally believed to reside on mountains, in ancient Near Eastern mythology. YHWH was no different. Jerusalem is God's holy city, the place where he dwells and, as such, is named Mount Zion, just as Baal's home in the Ugaritic texts is Mount Zaphon. The Temple is built to mirror God's heavenly home in a garden on a mountain top — hence its decorations of carved trees and plants.[25]

The fittings of the Temple all have symbolic value within a cosmic context. The Holy of Holies is the very place where God dwells; the veil separating it from the inner courts of the building was woven with the colours of the visible world to symbolize the human setting, as were the priestly garments worn for cultic activity in this area of the site. To go 'beyond the veil' the priest donned only a white linen garment, signifying the ascent into heaven, entry to the divine presence itself. The throne of God has already been mentioned; it remains to say that it fits into this 'symbolic universe' as a symbol of the deity's living existence with the worshippers at the Temple. To see the throne is to be before God, as evidenced by texts such as Daniel 7 and Ezekiel 1.[26]

Underlying the value given to symbolic items in the Temple is a particular concept of time and space. In this framework there is no gap between ordinary daily life and eternal time and space. The Temple and its fittings are simultaneously simply human artefacts *and* heavenly realities. Time and space are experienced as present reality, but they exist in the shadow of heaven — hence the OT definition of the world as 'heavens and earth'.[27] The Temple is the crossover, the bridge between heaven and earth and hence the central point of the universe, viewed as the tip of the high mountain on which God dwells part in heaven and part on earth. The role of mythology is to communicate this level of understanding to human audiences; Barker claims that the OT certainly fulfils this function:

The myths of Israel ... were a world view ... One lived in relation to them, knowing that they affected life just as much as our knowledge of gravity limits what any sane person will attempt to do.[28]

The Temple was not simply an empty showcase, a symbolic building sufficient unto itself. It was a suitable setting for human religious activity, aiding these cultic actions, making them effective both in heaven and on earth. The nature and significance of cultic acts carried out in sacred space is the subject of R. Murray's book *The Cosmic Covenant*.[29] Like Barker, Murray draws on a number of texts from different parts of the OT and from non-canonical Jewish books in order to support and illustrate his argument. He begins with the theme of OT theology. What is the content of this phrase? Murray does not claim to have found *the* answer here, but he does argue that it is possible to detect an underlying coherence to the OT collection which can be described as symbiosis of God, human beings and the universe, hence cosmic covenant.[30]

Murray turns first to the topic of the initial covenant, that established by God in creation: 'This aspect ... pictures God, in the process of creation, imposing a boundary ... and rules ... on the unruly elements.'[31]

This can be seen in Job 38:8–11, for example. Further information can be gleaned from the book of *Enoch* where the text refers to God binding the heavenly forces by a Great Oath:

One feature in this fusion of old traditions in *1 Enoch* 69 which is not found in its biblical sources is the Name by the power of which God bound the elements. In 69:13–14 it is the name of the oath, while God controls the elements by knowing their names.[32]

Chapters 1–4 of Murray's book trace two themes connected with the initial cosmic covenant, that of breach of order and that of re-establishment. This may remind the reader of our discussion in Chapter 2 of the three images of God in Genesis 1 – 11. God as creator establishes order. But somehow there are forces of disorder at work which undo divine harmony. These are represented in Genesis as human wrong choices and inadequate wisdom and in *1 Enoch* as supernatural disobedience by fallen angels. This breach of cosmic order results in divine judgement which itself unties the binding by oath and allows watery chaos full play in the Flood. But God regains control of the elements and establishes an eternal order which once more brings fertility to land and prosperity to humans. Murray's account of these themes looks at the cosmic upheaval pictured in Isaiah 24 – 27[33] and at the re-ordering of cosmic relations in Hosea,[34] for instance.

Chapter 5 then focuses on the function of cult within this ideological framework. Human success is the product of divine ordering and can be maintained only by the continuation of divine assistance but order is constantly under threat. The weather might change and the rains fail, leading to drought and death. Or a plague of locusts might sweep down on the crops and devour them. Or a neighbouring society might invade one's boundaries, plundering and destroying. All these evils and many more are breaches of cosmic order. They need to be averted. Temple rituals were designed to meet these social needs. There is no surviving handbook of Israelite ritual for the reader to study, but traces of ritual action can be found in the OT, Murray claims.[35] These rituals were part of the daily life of a kingdom and the Israelite / Judaean kings were probably central actors on the stage of cultic drama, just as Solomon is the key figure in the account of the consecration of the Temple in 1 Kings 8.

It is suggested, therefore, that 'control rituals' may have been performed ... These had two sides (a) actions to counter and control hostile forces by cursing them and enacting their ruin, and (b) the establishment of *shalom* by appropriate symbolic action and by affirming the universal rule of *sedeq* [justice] in heaven and on earth.[36]

Both Barker and Murray make use of non-biblical texts for their understanding of the significance of the Temple. Some of these can be found in a book compiled by C. T. R. Hayward.[37] Hayward takes the main Jewish sources for information about the Second Temple which are not to be found in the Hebrew Scriptures and presents them in an English translation, together with a short commentary. Here may be examined major evidence for the influence of Temple ideology on early Jewish thought — works such as the book of *Jubilees* and the writings of the first-century CE Jewish authors Philo of Alexandria and Josephus.

It is clear, from the above examination of the background to Ezekiel, that Temple ideology was an important means of explaining the nature of the deity and of his relationship to humans and to the universe. This ideology included, on the one hand, a mythological perspective on the world and its creator, and, on the other hand, a means of moral measurement which would bring society into line with the transcendent deity. It is this latter aspect which features so largely in the prophet's account of God's dealings with himself and with the people. The Temple is the place where the identity of God is revealed; it is also the place from which divine judgement issues. One Jerusalem Temple ceases to be capable of that role since the priests within it have lost sight of their true religious values. But that is not the end of the Temple. So strong is its pull on the writer of Ezekiel that he is drawn to believe in a future Temple pure enough to fulfil its timeless purpose of bringing together the heavens and the earth.

Summary

Ezekiel is the focus for the final study of God in prophetic works. This is a priestly book whose messages are drawn from, and relate to, the Temple in Jerusalem. First of all the nature of this priestly vocabulary is explored, then two themes are developed which go deeper into the image of God and Temple. These are the theme of holiness / purity and the mythology connected with Mount Zion.

Notes

1   In fact the date of Ezekiel is much debated and there is support for the view that it was written in the Persian period rather than in the Babylonian Exile. For

more information on this matter see the commentary by H. McKeating: *Ezekiel* (Sheffield: Sheffield Academic Press, 1993).

2 For more information on the strangeness of the book see McKeating (1993), ch. 3.

3 See, for instance, the account of the fall of Jericho in Joshua 6.

4 Tremper Longman III and D. G. Reid, *God Is a Warrior* (Carlisle: Paternoster, 1995), pp. 40–1.

5 The initial vision of the throne-chariot introduces the action of the first part of the book since the prophet is now inspired to view Jerusalem and the Temple as corrupt and to prophesy its doom.

6 See the animal fable in *1 Enoch* 84–90. In this account Israel are sheep, its great heroes and leaders are bulls or rams and angelic messengers are given human form. Thus, in chapter 87, there emerges from heaven a 'snow-white person' (translation from J. H. Charlesworth (ed.), *The Old Testament Pseudepigrapha*, vol. I (London: Darton, Longman & Todd / New York: Doubleday, 1983), p. 63).

7 See Leviticus 8, for instance, together with the account of the establishment of cult in Exodus 28 – 29.

8 P. Joyce, *Divine Initiative and Human Response in Ezekiel* (Sheffield: Sheffield Academic Press, 1989).

9 Joyce (1989), p. 90.

10 Joyce (1989), p. 103.

11 J. F. A. Sawyer (ed.), *Reading Leviticus: A Conversation with Mary Douglas* (Sheffield: Sheffield Academic Press, 1996).

12 J. Milgrom, 'The changing concept of holiness in the pentateuchal codes with emphasis on Leviticus 19' in Sawyer (ed.) (1996).

13 Milgrom (1996), p. 66.

14 Milgrom (1996), p. 67.

15 Milgrom (1996), p. 74.

16 M. Douglas, 'Sacred contagion' in Sawyer (ed.) (1996).

17 Douglas (1996), p. 92.

18 Douglas (1996), p. 96.

19 This is distinct from prophetic mode, where the prophet stands for purity against the defilement of the nation. Priests will be subject to impurity where their bodily functions and conditions are involved and must be cleansed of this defilement like any other human being.

20 Douglas (1996), pp. 97–9.

21 Douglas (1996), p. 106.

22 M. Barker, *The Gate of Heaven* (London: SPCK, 1991).

23 Barker (1991), ch. 1.

24 Barker (1991), ch. 2.

25 Barker (1991), pp. 68–70.

26 Barker (1991), ch. 3.

27 This is the typical phrase in the OT for the cosmos; it defines the whole entity by its two opposing poles. Thus Genesis 1 opens 'In the beginning when God created the heavens and the earth ...'.

28 Barker (1991), p. 180.

29 R. Murray, *The Cosmic Covenant* (London: Sheed & Ward, 1992).

30 Murray (1992), Introduction.

31 Murray (1992), p. 2.

32 Murray (1992), p. 11.

33 Murray (1992), pp. 16–22.
34 Murray (1992), pp. 27–32.
35 Murray (1992), pp. 68–70.
36 Murray (1992), p. 75.
37 C. T. R. Hayward, *The Jewish Temple* (London: Routledge, 1996).

Section C
Writings

9 *God and Divine Wisdom*

This study of images of God in the Old Testament turns now from prophecy to the third section of the Hebrew Scriptures, that of the (Other) Writings. This is a mixed collection of texts, lacking the coherence of Torah or Prophecy. The next three chapters will examine the images of the deity to be found in different subsections of this material — that of Wisdom books, Psalms and Apocalypse.

This chapter focuses on the god of the Wisdom tradition. The term Wisdom tradition is the title which contemporary scholarship has given to the three Hebrew texts Proverbs, Job and Qohelet (Ecclesiastes), and to two Jewish texts from the third to first centuries BCE, Sirach (Ecclesiasticus) and Wisdom of Solomon, now existing in Greek versions. Only the Hebrew books are found in the Jewish Bible. Modern scholars view these books as evidence of a coherent attitude to the world and to God which can be labelled 'Wisdom'. The name 'Wisdom' is taken from the books themselves which both describe the content of the human quality, wisdom, and also reflect on the divine aspects of this concept.

Wisdom — Hebrew *hokmah*, Greek *sophia* — is a word found generally in the OT. As a basic term it covers a range of meanings from the skills of a craftsman to the justice of a ruler to the learning of a wise man (*hakam*) or sage. In all these meanings it expresses a viewpoint on human existence. It is an advantage for a society to have wise leaders who can govern well, for instance. Hence the emphasis on Solomon as the ideal wise king: one who seeks wisdom before wealth and becomes the repository of knowledge about the world of his day.[1] Psalms also reflect on the value of being wise as against foolish. Psalm 14 is a clear example of this approach with humans divided into two classes of being, the wise and the fools. The fools do not believe that the divine sphere has any real influence on their lives and will come to great terror because of this attitude. A text which reflects a range of meaning attached to wisdom is Sirach 38:24 – 39:11. Here the wisdom of the scribe is set against the wisdom of farmers and craftsmen. Each has a necessary and important skill, but the text endorses the value of learning and meditation above the other forms of wisdom.

The content of the concept 'wisdom', however, is not produced by a random usage of the term throughout the OT, but is focused by the existence of the five books of the Wisdom tradition. The three Hebrew texts each have their own coherent, though sometimes paradoxical, message to offer. Proverbs appears, at first sight, to be a loosely federated collection of individual two-line sayings prefaced by several chapters of discourse. However, a tighter meaning emerges on closer examination. By the use of Hebrew poetry with its two-line repetitions and balances an overall argument is constructed. Chapter 15, for instance, focuses on the themes of mouth, tongue, eye and mind. The use of parallel images, such as tongue and lips for mouth, both opens up the text and yet maintains a common thread of meaning through the verses. These aspects of the human body stand for the whole person;[2] they can be used properly through the discreet use of speech, or badly through impulsive and thoughtless utterance. Proper and improper usage applies to all aspects of the human being, including reason and mind. The text builds up in this manner the message that there are two classes of human beings, wise and foolish. It is better to be wise since life's advantages fall to such people in the end. Proverbs, then, is an optimistic text since it aims to tell young men[3] how to lead useful lives, how to win friends and influence people.

By contrast Job and Qohelet seem much more gloomy about the scope of human knowledge. Is it really so easy to define right and wrong conduct? Or even to see the workings of a just supernatural order in the events of daily life? Qohelet is famous for his signature tune 'Vanity of vanities', says the Preacher, 'all is vanity'. Job, meanwhile, debates the sufferings of an innocent man and the unpredictability of divine support of faithful worshippers. All three books offer matter for reflection and instruction. Those who study them are students of wisdom. Wisdom here implies the human level of perception of the world, what Qohelet describes as an 'under the sun' perspective. God is a reality inherently part of the universe, a being whose existence can be surmised from the workings of world order. This makes the deity more of a remote principle of order than the personal friend of Israel's heroes — the type of god found in Torah and Prophecy. In these three books no attention is given to the theme of exodus or land settlement. The image of the deity is closer to that of the wisdom literature of other ancient societies such as Egypt and Mesopotamia.[4]

At its broadest extent wisdom is an attitude to existence, both secular and religious. These two dimensions are not separate but interweave with each other. God is to be found within the universe; the universe takes its true meaning from the existence of a divine overlord. Job 28 is typical of this mixed perspective. The text asks where wisdom is to be found. It points out that human beings have skills beyond those of the chief of birds, the eagles, or the king of beasts, the lion. Human skill brings to light hidden treasures from the mines of the earth, jewels brought back from deep darkness. But can humans mine wisdom? The chapter offers an emphatic 'No'. So where can wisdom be found? It is not found in earth or sea, though Death and the Underworld have heard of it.[5] In the end wisdom belongs to God alone since only he knows the full story of the universe, being its creator. It is this deity who tells humanity that, for them, wisdom is to have a religious attitude (fear of the Lord).

In the aspects dealt with so far wisdom is an object — a quality which human beings can have. But within the five Wisdom books as a whole another face of wisdom emerges. In this approach wisdom is not object but subject. Wisdom is a female who cries out in the streets and accompanies God in creation. Thus another image of God in the OT is that of Divine Wisdom. A number of issues have been raised about this image among modern scholars who have an interest in the figure of Wisdom; it is, for instance, a significant topic among feminine commentators who see in this image a possibility of rooting the dignity of women in God's own self.

Before examining the issues raised it is necessary to look at the passages which arouse the comments and to explore their content. Proverbs 1 − 9 appears to be a separate subsection of the text, being composed of continuous discourse rather than individual sayings. Proverbs 1:20 introduces Lady Wisdom who cries out in the city streets, looking for the wise among the citizens who will heed her advice. Chapter 8 picks up this theme, while chapter 9 adds on the theme of Wisdom's banquet. Wisdom has a house prepared for the comfort of those who will be invited in. These images of Lady Wisdom are balanced by the image of Dame Folly, the adulterous woman, in chapter 7. She also looks for clients, but brings the men concerned not life and joy but death and disaster.

It could be said of these word pictures that they use contemporary male experience of women as a literary tool to dramatize the message of the rest of the book. However, there is a further dimension to Lady Wisdom, to be found in chapter 8. Here Wisdom describes herself as a being related to God:

The Lord created me at the beginning of his work ... Ages ago I was set up, at the first, before the beginning of the earth ... (Prov 8:22–23)

When he established the heavens I was there ... when he marked out the foundations of the earth, then I was beside him, like a master worker.[6] (Prov 8:27–30)

The implication of these passages is that Wisdom is a heavenly being, one of great intimacy with God. This image of wisdom emerges also from the two Greek Wisdom books. In Sirach 24 Wisdom praises herself at the heavenly court, thus clearly claiming the role of supernatural being:

I came forth from the mouth of the Most High ... my throne was in a pillar of cloud ... Over the waves of the sea, over all the earth, and over every people ... I have held sway ... (Sir 24:3–6)

Wisdom seeks a dwelling on earth and is told by God to rest with Israel and to be its guide. The practical face of this incarnation is the literature of instruction, the Torah (verse 23). Just as Wisdom set up her table in Proverbs so now the food of Torah is sweeter than honey (verse 20). Later in the book the great heroes of Israel are said to be indwelt by wisdom and so inspired to do their work (chapter 44 onwards). Thus Israel's sacred traditions are interwoven with wisdom language, a development from the three Hebrew texts.

The Wisdom of Solomon also links wisdom with a divine being. In chapter 6 a figure who appears to be King Solomon prays to God and Wisdom is sent down from heaven as his marriage partner. The speaker now praises Wisdom, utilizing the language of Greek philosophy, calling her

a spirit that is intelligent, holy, unique, manifold, subtle ... a breath of the power of God, and a pure emanation of the glory of the Almighty ... a spotless mirror of the working of God ... (Wis 7:22–26)

How then are these images of divine wisdom to be interpreted by the reader? The base note is that connected with the image of God. Is God accompanied by a female deity of some sort, for instance? Or is wisdom envisaged as an attribute of the deity which has a somewhat separate existence? J. McKinlay[7] summarizes the possibilities envisaged by scholars. She refers to J. Dunn who points out that whereas polytheism would allow for an independent being, the kind of monotheism evidenced in the final layer of the editing of the OT makes any independent divinity problematic. One can only argue for a hypostatization, that is, a semi-separate facet of divine being, a quality which has shape and purpose in itself, as viewed from the human perspective, without in fact implying a second being, existing quite independently:

Definitions have included Mowinckel's half independent, half revelatory form, ... and Ringgren's quasi-personification of certain attributes of God,[8]

while Von Rad 'argued that while wisdom is indeed personified, that personification is not limited to an attribute of Yahweh',[9] but must be applied more widely to personification of concepts. This argument, however, in the end comes to the same conclusion, as do all theories of semi-separate attributes. They hang somewhat uneasily between twoness and oneness, within the framework of human number concepts.

In order to explore the matter more deeply it is necessary to situate the text in its social context — in this case, the culture of the ancient Near East. One possibility of divine Wisdom is that behind the text lies an actual goddess. Two alternative settings here are that of Syro-Palestinian religion of the ninth to eighth century BCE and that of Hellenistic religion of the third to first century BCE. If the OT as it now stands reflects the Hellenistic world-view, then Wisdom can be compared to oriental deities such as the Egyptian Isis. Isis texts exist which show the goddess proclaiming her own achievements as a patroness of human life, in a literary style called aretalogy. Sirach 24 could be a deliberate imaging of the Isis texts which transfers the source of world order from Egyptian to Jewish culture. As E. Schüssler Fiorenza remarks:

Several scholars have suggested that Hellenistic Jewish wo/men in Egypt conceived of Divine Wisdom as prefigured in the language and image of Goddesses like Isis, Athena, or Dike ... Like Isis, Sophia is called upon as Divine Saviour.[10]

The presence of Sophia-Isis in the Wisdom texts offers feminist scholars like Schüssler Fiorenza the opportunity for a religious base which does not view the deity totally as a male being. From this base Christian feminists interrogate New Testament Christology, seeking to reveal the Wisdom aspect of the image of Jesus, from Matthew, for instance, where Jesus follows Wisdom's words inviting people 'to come and learn from me'.[11]

However, if Wisdom belongs to the Hellenistic level of the OT she belongs within a monotheistic religion. This makes her dependent on YHWH, a male deity; ultimately she is subsumed within that god. She is only a breath from God's mouth or the channel of his creative acts. It has been argued that the development of attributes within the godhead is the way monotheism copes with the need to make one god the source of many different actions in the universe. There is some tension between a male godhead and a female wisdom, but that can be overcome by arguing that neither the term 'male' nor 'female' has everyday language values here. God is above gender values, being totally spiritual, disembodied. But McKinlay remarks in this context:

For people living as gendered persons in gendered society the reality, whether desirable or not, appears much closer to that expressed by Rita Goss ...

The metaphor of a gender-free person is impossible. Persons are male and female.[12]

McKinlay's study, indeed, examines the manner in which the figure of Wisdom begins in Proverbs as an individual female, but in Sirach has been brought under male control. Wisdom is told by God where to dwell and, as incarnated in Torah, becomes the possession of the male scribe who tells the story of the book.[13] The explanation of Wisdom from the setting of Hellenistic religion, then, focuses on a single divine figure, YHWH, who has chosen to relate to creation through semi-separable divine attributes, one of which is the power of reason and understanding.

It is possible to view Wisdom as goddess from another angle, that of an earlier period in the development of Yahwism. In this explanation Wisdom is an echo of a once well-known and loved goddess within Israelite polytheism. She is to be identified with the figure of Asherah, a person referred to in OT texts and traceable within archaeological remains of the ninth century BCE.[14] McKinlay gives a thorough and neutral account of the resource material connected with Asherah in her first chapter.[15] The OT evidence is puzzling, for Asherah sometimes appears to be a cult symbol such as a tree or a pillar of wood and sometimes appears to be a deity. As cult symbol Asherah is attacked by the Deuteronomists, who link this symbol with Baal worship and demand the cutting down and burning of the offending objects.[16] As a deity Asherah may be the goddess Jeremiah refers to as Queen of Heaven, whose cult he objects to among the women of Jerusalem.[17] Outside the OT a number of cult statues of female deities have been excavated in Judaean ruins and the Kuntillet Arjud inscription appears to refer to Yahweh and his Asherah. Here there is material which can be interpreted to mean that Asherah was a local goddess in Israel, or which can be evaluated as uncertain in its implications. One scholar who has taken up this debate is M. Barker.

Barker's book *The Great Angel*[18] contains a chapter on the evidence about Wisdom. Barker's overall argument is Christological, but she leads to this by pointing out aspects of OT theology which have ongoing effects on Christian thought. Barker raises the question about a goddess hidden within the OT texts. She points out that Philo in the first century CE knew of the idea that the cherubim of YHWH had two faces, one male and one female.[19] From this piece of evidence Barker moves on to rehearse the textual evidence connected with the name Asherah (material covered also by McKinlay's first chapter). She argues that there is enough material to allow the reader to posit the original existence of a creatress-consort alongside YHWH. Although this figure has an individual role to play in the world order, she is not a fully separate being but points to a certain androgyny within the godhead. Some of the Asherah material within biblical texts links the goddess figure to a Tree of Life, source of nurture.[20] This has echoes of the Asherah symbol as tree or wooden pillar. Outside the OT some of the inscriptional evidence depicts a goddess as a tree between two lions.

Drawing on this evidence, Barker argues that the figure of Wisdom is not the reflection of a foreign woman imported at a later date, as in the Isis theory, but points rather to an originally Israelite figure, who was later marginalized as monotheism took over:

Being the creatress-consort and having the tree symbol are in themselves sufficient to link her to the later Wisdom figure who is described in just this way.[21]

Barker thus envisages Wisdom as the final traces of an original female divine personality. She argues that this figure was the other face of YHWH. Thus originally YHWH contained both male and female elements, as may be read from Genesis 1 where one explanation of the idea of humans made in the image of God is 'male and female'.[22]

M. Smith, also, provided a chapter on Asherah in his work on the nature of God in the OT.[23] He, too, rehearses the evidence, textual and otherwise, concerning Asherah and Israel. He, too, links her with the figure of Wisdom: 'Like the symbol of the asherah, Wisdom is a female figure, providing life and nurturing.'[24]

On the question of whether Asherah was an Israelite goddess, Smith feels that the evidence is unclear. He focuses on the symbol in the cult, rather, and argues that this offers a female aspect to YHWH after the period in which any actual goddess may have functioned in Israel. The Asherah symbol is assimilated to YHWH:

From ... survey of the biblical evidence, it would appear that the asherah continued with various functions in the cult of Yahweh without connection to the goddess who gave her name to the symbol.[25]

Smith sees the use of male and female images of God in Isaiah as evidence of the continuing influence of the Asherah figure on Israelite religion. The gradual fading out of the female side of YHWH he suggests was part of the wider move in post-exilic Yahwism to remove anthropomorphic language about the deity. This took place as one part of the move towards a single deity as the focus for religious belief in the Persian and Hellenistic periods.[26]

As can be gathered from the above account of scholarly work, the topic of a goddess as source for Lady Wisdom is a major concern for modern commentators. Part of this concern is the spin-off for the place of women in modern Jewish and Christian thought. God as a male deity, whether actively gendered or not, provides a rationale for men's control of women. A. Brenner has considered the figure of Wisdom in relation to women as a whole in the OT.[27] In *Israelite Woman* she surveys a number of female types in the OT from wise human women, to harlots, to mothers of heroes. It is within this broader field of the place of women in OT thought that both Lady Wisdom and Lady Folly are to be situated. The overall picture of women in the OT leads the reader to a mixed attitude about them. On the one hand women can be saviours of their nation, as with Judith and Esther. On the other, they can be destructive of social order, adulteresses tempting men into sin, as with Potiphar's wife in the Joseph story in Genesis.

The Wisdom tradition is equally ambivalent about women. Proverbs 31 pictures a worthy wife and mother running a super-efficient home, whereas Sirach seems to have a fear of daughters whose conduct shames their father. These various views are attached to female sexuality. It is the use of this by women which brings joy or sorrow to the men. Divine Wisdom is caught up into the same debate. Lady Wisdom builds a house and sets out a feast and is approved by the author of Proverbs. But Lady Folly does exactly the same works and yet is a trap and a snare. As Brenner comments:

It is paradoxical, then, that the wicked female death trap shares some important features with personified Wisdom, the fountain of life.[28]

The two figures each offer an invitation to come to their house and have compelling arguments as to why this invitation should be taken advantage of. But only one of the figures represents life. The close similarities between the two figures combined with one total distinction can only be resolved by giving one aspect prime importance. Thus, the image of the good woman is truer than that of the evil woman, or vice versa.

McKinlay also relates to the ambivalence connected with Divine Wisdom. She discusses the interaction between the image of Wisdom and images of women in Proverbs[29] and argues that, in the end, the independent active woman of Wisdom is deconstructed by the image of a hardworking domestic organizer:

It appears that within the book of Proverbs hymned Wisdom, who comes from intimate conversations ... with Yahweh to move apparently so independently in human disguise in the public places of the Israelite city, is first counterbalanced by the 'seductive woman' ... and is finally brought home as the incomparable wife, worthy beyond all others.[30]

One scholar who has spent much time studying Wisdom books is L. Perdue. His account of *Wisdom and Creation*[31] avoids direct discussion of the social setting of the image of God as Divine Wisdom. His text assumes the existence of a mythology in Israel in which goddesses figured. He then explains the images of Wisdom as tree and as fountain, for instance, as literary devices which take their meaning from pre-existent mythology.[32] Perdue's main argument is that the practical instructions of Wisdom books and the series of reflections on divine justice or the value of order come from a common root, a theology which undergirds all the books. This is the theology of creation. Divine Wisdom takes her identity from this context. Drawing on Mesopotamian myth concerning the battle between the gods and the creation of the universe from Tiamat, the defeated deity, Perdue sees Israelite Wisdom describing the balance between order and chaos in the universe. This order encompasses the world as a whole as well as human society and neighbourhood relations: 'Two forces ... contend for the rulership of the earth: life and death, Yahweh and Mot, ... Wisdom and Folly.'[33]

From this base Perdue offers a creation commentary on each of the five Wisdom books in turn, dealing with the image of Divine Wisdom as it emerges in a particular book. Since Perdue deals with the texts in a chronological order he is able to maintain the continuity of the female Divine Wisdom while also allowing for changes across time. The mythological background for Proverbs can be situated in a Syro-Palestinian religion which knew of Asherah, Ishtar and Anat, while that of Wisdom of Solomon can look rather to the Hellenistic world of Isis and Athena.

Since Perdue's intention is to highlight the worth of Wisdom literature and to retrieve it from its second-class status, lying behind Torah or Prophecy in value, he tends also to view Divine Wisdom from a positive angle. He notes the tendency of the Wisdom figure in the tradition to gather to itself increasing significance. Thus, in Wisdom of Solomon the divine female draws to herself the concept of spirit, which elsewhere in the OT is an independent attribute of the deity.[34] Wisdom, for instance, is the breath of God, that is, his Spirit in Solomon's song of praise for Divine Wisdom in chapters 6 – 7. In Sirach, Wisdom is equated with Torah and thus with divine Word. The term *dabar* (word) in Hebrew means also 'thing' or 'event'; that is its connotation in Torah where the Commandments are Word of God while at the same time requiring translation into human actions. The most positive literary evaluation of wisdom, in Wisdom, shows how

Woman wisdom permeates creation, holds it together, and provides it with a structure and order, while as the divine spirit she renews all life ... She is the embodiment of providence, identified with God's mind, which controls and directs the operations of the cosmos.[35]

Such a figure and the religious context which gives her meaning should, according to Perdue,

be a valued resource, not only for reconstructing ancient Israel ... but also for contributing to the contemporary articulations of believing communities seeking to describe their faith in coherent and meaningful ways.[36]

Ultimately, then, what value is the modern reader to place on this image of God in the OT as Divine Wisdom? One of the issues here is the link between this image and the development of religious thought in a tradition. Divine Wisdom may reflect both something of polytheistic imagery for divine characteristics in a situation where many individual deities offer a range of possible readings for the character of god and something of the challenge which a monotheistic perspective faces in claiming that all known aspects of divine character apply to one named God. The monotheistic aspect of this matter continues to exercise the minds of Christians since mainstream Christianity claims both one God and yet three persons within that God.

Another important subject for the modern reader is the place of femininity within the godhead. If god(s) form models for society, imaging its sense of order and identity, what place has the feminine within such social / divine models? In turn, what real value will be placed on women in the home, the market place, government and authority positions as a result of this image? Will the wisdom of women be given social power? Can women image God?

Summary

The last section of the book, dealing with the Writings part of the OT, begins with the Wisdom material. Whereas prophets address God through titles, the Wisdom material highlights another approach to the deity, that of divine attributes. God may be a single being but aspects of the divine reach out into creation and so achieve God's purpose within the universe. Lady Wisdom is one of these attributes. The chapter looks at the language within the OT which gives rise to this image and then at the scholarship which has arisen recently on the subject of the feminine within the godhead.

Notes

1   There are a series of expansions to the Solomon traditions. Solomon's wisdom comes to cover magical and healing knowledge as well as cosmological facts. The pentangle, known as Solomon's Seal, was a point of interest for Jewish, Christian and Islamic intellectuals in the medieval period. For more on the Solomon material see 'Testament of Solomon' in J. H. Charlesworth (ed.), *The Old Testament Pseudepigrapha* (London: Darton, Longman & Todd / New York: Doubleday, 1983, 1985), and the chapter on Solomon in M. E. Mills, *Human Agents of Cosmic Power* (Sheffield: Sheffield Academic Press, 1990).

2   This is a well-known technique of Wisdom literary style, known as metonymy, in which the part implies the whole to which it belongs. The message, then, is not about a tongue but about the human person understood through command of speech.

3   The Wisdom books typically take the form of an address of Father to 'my son'. This usage may reflect the origins of proverbial teaching in the family home and/or it may reflect the formal style of opening a lecture adopted by sages at

royal courts. The addressees are always men, usually young men who have to learn what life is about in order to make a public career for themselves and run households well.

4 Many commentators note the cosmopolitan nature of wisdom books. Close parallels to Proverbs exist in Egyptian royal instructions and similar ideas to Job and Qohelet can be found in Mesopotamian texts such as *The Babylonian Theodicy*. For a good general introduction to aspects of wisdom see R. Murphy, 'Introduction to wisdom literature' in R. Brown, J. Fitzmyer and R. Murphy (eds), *The New Jerome Biblical Commentary* (Englewood Cliffs, NJ: Prentice-Hall / London: Geoffrey Chapman, 1989).

5 Death and Abaddon are linked in this verse. The text shows signs of mythological imagery since, in Ugarit, Death (Mot) was a god who fought Baal for control of the world. Abaddon appears to be the equivalent of OT Sheol or the Pit.

6 The text has two possibilities here — child or craftsman, depending on the actual Hebrew word. Commentators differ as to translation. For an account of the problem see L. G. Perdue, *Wisdom and Creation: The Theology of Wisdom Literature* (Nashville: Abingdon, 1994), p. 91, for some discussion of the matter.

7 J. E. McKinlay, *Gendering Wisdom the Host* (Sheffield: Sheffield Academic Press, 1996).

8 McKinlay (1996), p. 78.

9 McKinlay (1996), p. 79.

10 E. Schüssler Fiorenza, *Jesus, Miriam's Child, Sophia's Prophet* (London: SCM Press, 1994), p. 136.

11 See Matthew 11:28–30.

12 McKinlay (1996), p. 242.

13 McKinlay (1996), p. 158.

14 Reference to Asherah alone is just one aspect of the wider topic of exactly which goddesses were worshipped in ancient Syro-Palestine and the extent to which several figures overlapped. If wisdom is a key value, the Asherah, Astarte and Anath are all goddesses of the region associated with that quality. For more detail see, for instance, M. Smith, *The Early History of God* (New York: Harper & Row, 1990), ch. 3.

15 See note 7 above.

16 As in, e.g., Deuteronomy 7:5.

17 See, e.g., Jeremiah 44:17–18.

18 M. Barker, *The Great Angel* (London: SPCK, 1992).

19 Barker (1992), p. 48.

20 Barker (1992), p. 58.

21 Barker (1992), p. 58.

22 The report of God's speech in Genesis 1 allows for two meanings to 'Let us make Adam in our image'. One of these is to have power and dominion, i.e. the image of kingship, but the other is the image of gender. 'Let us make' is followed by 'male and female he created them'.

23 See note 14 above.

24 Smith (1990), p. 95.

25 Smith (1990), p. 94.

26 Smith (1990). This discussion extends over pp. 97–103.

27 A. Brenner, *The Israelite Woman: Social Role and Literary Type* (Sheffield: Sheffield Academic Press, 1994).

28 Brenner (1994), p. 44.
29 McKinlay (1996) covers this subject in two separate chapters, one for Wisdom and one for women in Proverbs.
30 McKinlay (1996), p. 131.
31 See note 6 above.
32 Perdue (1994), pp. 82 and 272 respectively.
33 Perdue (1994), p. 100.
34 Wisdom as attribute of God fits within a much wider topic concerning divine attributes in the OT. The three well-known qualities are Word, Wisdom, Spirit. These are thought to prefigure the Trinitarian understanding of God in the Christian tradition. Each of the three terms deserves its own chapter. Further information on Word and Spirit can be found in G. Kittel (ed.), *Theological Dictionary of the New Testament* (Grand Rapids: Eerdmans/London: SCM Press, 1964–71), under 'Logos' and 'Pneuma' respectively.
35 Perdue (1994), p. 321.
36 Perdue (1994), p. 342.

10 God of power and justice in Psalms

The previous chapter discussed the issue of Divine Wisdom, taking Wisdom here as an attribute of the deity. An attribute in this context is an aspect of divine outreach to the created world. God remains outside creation, the author of life itself. However, God is not totally outside human knowledge in the OT, since divine energy continues to act upon created matter, shaping and moulding it into divinely-ordained order. There are channels, then, through which divine power operates and which can be identified by humans. In the OT the three dominant channels of God's power are Wisdom, Word and Spirit. They express the idea of a deity who thinks and plans in a logical manner, who gives expression to that rational purpose in speech — particularly in command language — and whose energy flows out to carry through the actions commanded and purposed.[1]

In addition to the three main channels of communication used by God in the OT, there are other focuses of divine action. God's name, for instance, can be called upon to access the power of the deity.[2] Speech can include the concept of 'oath', a binding promise which God swore to in the past and which still determines his activities.[3] All of these links between God and world reflect the powerfulness of God; they are expressions of that power. Power in itself can be a neutral term or may have positive or negative connotations. For example, an army leader controls weapons of considerable power which will be the source of defence for some people and death for others. Divine power also has a variety of possible effects. Moses uses that power to free Israelite slaves, but what the Egyptians experience is disaster and death (Exod 6 – 12).

Power can be viewed more positively when it is linked to the theme of justice. Power is then defined and controlled by just purposes. In the OT justice is usually paired with the term 'righteousness' and these two together are used as images of God. God is the source of order, of law and commandment and so of justice and righteousness. God's powerfulness and justice is a topic frequently at issue in the Writings, in the book of Psalms. Thus, for instance, Psalm 97 celebrates the reign of God:

Clouds and thick darkness are all around him; righteousness and justice are the foundation of his throne. (v. 2)

In Psalm 98 this theme leads to the hope for God's justice on earth:

he will judge the world with righteousness, and the peoples with equity. (v. 9)

It is not surprising that psalms contain so much information about the image of a god of power and justice since they were originally liturgical hymns performed in the cultic drama, for instance in the Temple in Jerusalem.[4] Sacred worship focuses on two themes, that of praise and that of petition.[5] Both moods lead the worshipper to dwell on the powerfulness of God. For either God is to be praised for the manner in which his power has been used to aid the worshipper's cause or God is to be implored to bring divine power into action to rescue and defend the petitioner.

Psalms are thus a useful resource for exploring OT images of God. This is not because the psalm collection in the Writings section of the OT has been formed into a tightly structured theological treatise. Each hymn or poem remains separate with its own vocabulary and internal structure of lines and verses. These texts are useful as a broad reflection of the styles in which the compilers of the OT envisioned the deity. Since the texts are addressed to God they convey a number of images consonant with the deity as source and origin of created existence and of historical events. The images cannot necessarily be pinned down as to exact date and authorship just as the psalms themselves cannot be tied to any one century but may represent the accumulation of worship material over several centuries. The cultic background of the texts is often reflected in the mythological language of the psalms; in particular the sovereignty of God is expressed through the idea of storm-theophany, as in the verse from Psalm 97 which was quoted above.

One of the major developments of psalm research in the twentieth century has been the situating of texts in a dynamic of active liturgy. This work was begun by H. Gunkel who moved from psalms as spiritual reading to speculating on the role of psalms in Israelite liturgy at temple or shrine.[6] His approach was taken further by S. Mowinckel, who examined the psalms in the context of what is known of cult and mythology in other cultures of the ancient Near East. In particular Mowinckel focused on the image of God as king and on the possibility of divine enthronement ceremonies as part of Israelite worship.[7] The work of R. Murray and of M. Barker, referred to in an earlier chapter, links with this manner of debating psalms. Murray's delineation of a cosmic covenant theme connects with the use of psalms as words capable of carrying through the ideas they contain in everyday affairs. Since the psalmist addresses God in praise for divine wonders of order or in dismay at a disruption of a visible world order, the role of the psalm is to endorse that which is good for the psalmist's world and correct that which is bad. Barker's account of the ideology connected with Temple cult provides the cultural context for understanding much of the vocabulary of psalms. The voice of the psalmist acclaiming the presence of God, for instance, as in Psalm 99: 'The Lord ... sits enthroned upon the cherubim', is a response to the cultic context of the Jerusalem Temple where the Lord of Israel has a throne-chariot, the Ark of the Lord. God is not only seated in the heavens but is also enthroned in the earthly Temple in the symbolism of cult objects.

In this approach the shrine of the Lord is the site of divine power and justice. A recent commentary on Psalms by J. C. McCann[8] dwells on this topic in the chapter on God's space and God's time. He takes Psalm 48 as his focus, drawing out from that text the idea of sacred space represented by Jerusalem. McCann points out that the meaning here is not simply the power of a human town but rather this town as a geographical metaphor:

Jerusalem, a seemingly ordinary place, has become to the eye of faith 'the city of the great king' (verse 2), a powerful symbol of God's reign in all places ... and in all times.[9]

The ultimate effect of this metaphorical code is to convey to the reader the belief that God's power is invincible, that no power on earth, no passage of time, can thwart the just purposes of the deity.[10] This view is deepened by McCann's treatment of two further psalms, Psalm 122 and Psalm 90. These texts deal with God's space and time, respectively. Psalm 122 denotes Jerusalem as a place of peace. Symbolically the city represents the unity and harmony which surround the deity. At its heart are the thrones of justice and from that justice blessing flows out to all those connected with the city. This is ideal space, one in which human beings live in direct contact with divine power and thus have an ordered and fruitful environment.

Psalm 90 focuses on the idea of time as an aspect of divine power and authority. All the days of human existence are within God's control and purpose. Divine knowledge of time and use of it operate on a wider plane than do human knowledge and use of time. This could give rise to a concept of an arbitrary divine ruler who suddenly cuts off human time (verses 11–12). But the theme of the text moves rather to God's use of time for compassionate judgement. Humans never have enough time to order their affairs properly — they run out of the commodity. But God can move time around and so bring positive human intentions to fulfilment beyond human expectations and yet within human hopes:

What the psalmist saw in Jerusalem was a sign that 'the Lord is here', amid the dark daily realities of a dying world, a world where nothing ever works out completely right and we are never all that we can be.[11]

The interweaving of the meaning of psalms in their original cultural background with their contribution to the religious teaching of the OT collection of religious books is a further aspect of modern scholarship. McCann addresses this issue at the start of his commentary. He picks up on a statement made by Muilenburg that attention should be given to the literary structure of the OT text in order to examine the message of the literary piece under examination, a process known as rhetorical criticism.[12] This enables the reader to understand the function of psalms as Torah or Instruction. In their present state the Psalms are part of a particular grouping of works and themselves show some signs of conscious editing:

Wilson, Childs and others have noted that psalm 1 forms an introduction to the psalter, the effect of which is ... that the psalter is not merely a collection of liturgical resources but is to be read and heard as a source of ... teaching.[13]

The message of Psalm 1 in this context is that God is the focal point of human experience. All human philosophies of life are to be measured against the divine purpose. Thus the authority of the deity gives a moral shape to life, 'for the Lord watches over the way of the righteous, but the way of the wicked will perish' (Ps 1:6).

It is reasonable, then, to turn attention to the theology of the Psalms, as J. Day has done.[14] He takes as his beginning the practical nature of psalm theology. The psalmist condemns those who would deny that the deity has any real impact on human experience. God is viewed as an active force in human affairs. Thus the Lord of Israel is celebrated as creator and as judge. The divine judgement extends not only to human conduct but also to other members of the Heavenly Council as in Psalm 82. Once again the background here is that of mythology.[15] The basis for divine authority to make these judgements is that of the great splendours of creation. The God who is responsible for such great works (as celebrated in the great creation Psalm 103–104, for instance) must be powerful above all possible rivals for cosmic power. The world is constantly kept in being in Psalm 103–104 by the abiding presence of the Lord with his works; thus God in psalms is both 'in here' and 'out there'. His authority unites heaven and earth. This authority is connected with certain divine qualities such as lovingkindness or *hesed*:

Altogether [*hesed*] occurs [in Psalms] over one hundred times. It is variously translated as steadfast love, mercy, loyalty ... and denotes Yahweh's characteristic attitude towards the Israelites.[16]

God reveals the merciful side of his powerful nature by his interventions in the history of Israel, a topic also celebrated in Psalms. Most of all what is remembered is the exodus from Egypt and the crossing of the Red Sea when God overthrew Pharaoh and all his chariots in the midst of the waters (Pss 114, 135, 136, for instance). The theme which gathers all these theologies together is that of the kingship of God — a theme connected with the enthronement of YHWH at the Feast of Tabernacles.[17]

In the ancient Near East power in human society was most often associated with one great leader figure. This might be a war leader, a chieftain, a prince or a king. The OT includes texts which describe David as God's chosen leader for Israel and which view the Davidic kings as appointed to stand in God's place at the head of society. Psalm 72, for example, requests that God give the king true justice so that he can rule the people in an orderly manner which includes both social justice and the fertility of the land. The deity, it is implied, is the true ruler and source of social order, standing behind the human king. In a study of the kingship of God M. Brettler[18] discussed the manner of presenting God in the OT. Many qualities of human power are attached to God and flesh out the image of God here. These include:

- royal appellations such as Shepherd
- royal qualities such as wisdom, wealth
- royal trappings such as sceptre and throne
- the domestic setting of a king's court
- royal enthronement[19]

Brettler's study shows that divine kingship is closely modelled on human rulers. However, God's power is always superior to that of human rulers. God is all-mighty or all-knowing, for instance.[20] On the other hand, terms which indicate a lesser royal status are not applied to God. These include Messiah, a figure consecrated by another, and Branch or Stump which implies dependency on something else.

McCann also refers to the subject of the kingship of God.[21] Psalm 2, he argues, sets the scene for the psalter's approach to this topic: 'Psalm 2 should be heard primarily as an affirmation of God's sovereignty.'[22]

McCann believes that the first two psalms in the psalter establish the pattern for reading the other psalm texts: 'The psalms call persons to live under the reign of God, to "take refuge in" God.'[23] In his view the centrality of the image of god of power and justice is established right here at the very start of the hymn collection and is then illustrated and deepened in the following texts.

J. L. Mays[24] picks out the kingship of God as the strand which holds the psalm collection together. Mays takes from texts the phrase *YHWH malak*, translated as 'God is king' or 'God reigns'. He argues that the image of God as king was intended to communicate easily with an ancient audience. However this is problematic for a modern audience whose societies may not value kingship or may not have kings at all.[25] The way round this problem is to pass behind what kings did in the ancient world to the metaphor of power lying beyond actual daily experience of royal authority:

it is a term for a dynamic sovereignty ... administered in two patterns ... One is the pattern of ordering chaos to bring forth cosmos and world. The other is a scenario of intervening in human disorder by judgement and deliverance.[26]

This makes the Psalms into the liturgy of the kingdom of God since they constantly refer to the dynamism of divine rule. There are several aspects of this liturgy. The Psalms start with the kingship of God in creation. By defeating the many waters of chaos the Lord takes power, as in Psalm 93. It is this primeval royal act which is celebrated in divine enthronement psalms and in the acclamation 'God reigns!':

- As sovereign, YHWH has a special people, the congregation of Israel
- As sovereign, YHWH has a special place in the world, Zion is its name
- As sovereign, YHWH has a special person, his king, David
- As sovereign, YHWH orders the lives of his people by decrees, word, covenant[27]

These are the categories of royal power which Mays describes and to which he posits a human response:

- the praise in the Psalms is the voice of the servants of YHWH, who know him to be God of gods and Lord of lords
- the prayers in the Psalms appeal to YHWH as king and Lord of those who pray
- the Psalms base their teaching on the meaning of YHWH's reign for the conduct of life [28]

In this interpretation of the image of a god of power in Psalms Mays tries to bridge the gap between the culture of the original audience and that of contemporary society. His aim is to allow the texts to communicate the theology of their ancient compilers to a very different political and social context. Mays wishes to prevent the theme of divine kingship from being a block to understanding the nature of God, to turn it round so that it is visibly the linchpin on which the whole message of Psalms turns.

A move which is made by commentators like Mays is to broaden the image of divine kingship to the image of power. The term 'power' is connected, in the OT, with concepts of justice and right government. Kings have power in order to set up a just society, in order to be true shepherds of their peoples. The prophet Jeremiah, for instance, laments the failure of Israelite royal shepherds to act justly (Jer 23). A further image of a powerful God, then, is that of a just deity. The Psalms are a good area for researching this view of God, since the assumption of prayer is that a god exists who can answer the petitioner, and what petitioners often seek is justice, that is, the vindication of their cause. Thus Psalm 55 states:

But I call upon God, and the Lord will save me ... He will redeem me unharmed from the battle that I wage, for many are arrayed against me. (verses 16–18)

Mays argues, in this context, that the character and policy of YHWH's kingship shape the way in which the psalmist asks for help. God, he says, is

- one who delivers the weak
- who loves righteousness and justice, who supports the innocent
- who is compassionate to those who throw themselves on his mercy.

These characteristics of God allow the psalmist to call on God to arise and save the petitioners who cast their role in the form of an innocent person whose life is threatened by the violent oppression of others.[29] Mays suggests that the parallel to the God of justice is the human poor one, the righteous one. The attitude here is commonly one of human *ebed* (servant) to divine *adon* (master). Since this all-embracing image of righteousness binds God and petitioner together it can be used again and again, whatever the time frame or human life-style:

The prayers for salvation in the psalter became the poetry of this theological type. They are liturgy for all ... They deny any the right to speak as independent, autonomous, invulnerable, strong ... No one, they say, prays apart from his dependence and mortality.[30]

Righteousness fits into this theme since it addresses the well-being of the whole community and is connected with the common good, the peace and harmony of a society:

In the theological view of the psalms, righteousness belongs first to YHWH. His blessing and ordering give rightness to Israel's life. When the people ... are in trouble, his intervention to set things right is his righteousness.[31]

This is not language about self-justification on the part of humans, but rather formulaic vocabulary which gives voice to human dependency and need of compassion. The God of righteousness is a deity who encapsulates that neediness, whose energy reaching out into creation brings hope of renewal.

A further dimension to the image of divine righteousness is that of God the healer. M. L. Brown has written on this topic and has addressed the psalter in his study.[32] He argues that the Psalms function as a way of bringing the sickness of people to the deity's attention:

the proposition that Yahweh was the Healer of his people to whom they should readily come for deliverance was certainly well known, be it through the 'official' cultic religion or by means of 'popular / folk' beliefs.[33]

Healing and righteousness run together here, since sickness was regularly seen to denote the wrath of God breaking out on a person. Confession of sin and lament for sickness therefore form a common vocabulary in the Psalms: 'let the bones that you have crushed rejoice. Hide your face from my sins, and blot out all my iniquities' (Ps 51:8–9).

In response to this language God is described as one who heals: 'The Lord ... heals the brokenhearted, and binds up their wounds' (Ps 147:2–3); and this image is linked, in Psalm 146, with the concept of divine justice: 'Happy are those whose help is the God of Jacob ... who executes justice for the oppressed' (verse 7). In this the Lord of Israel shares a common feature with other ancient deities. Brown points to a hymn to Marduk the Babylonian god which describes him as a healer who has drawn a faithful worshipper from the river of destruction.[34]

God is both a deity who disciplines his followers through sickness and suffering and also a deity who favours those who worship him, bringing them back from sickness to health, from disaster to prosperity. There is a hint here of a less happy aspect to the God of power and justice, namely that of a god who deliberately causes pain. This possibility was referred to above, in the setting of divine control of history. Here it reappears in the guise of human suffering. There is common ground between the 'Lament Voice' of the Psalms and the voice of Job, for instance. Why does God not prevent pain, why does he let 'enemies' oppress the human being?[35] It is possible to reconcile pain and divine benevolence, perhaps by talking of the mysteriousness of God, as Job does, but the matter can also be taken on its own, as N. Whybray has done in an article on the immorality of God.[36] Whybray takes particular OT passages which show God acting in an unjust manner; God's giving in to the Satan's doubts at the start of the book of Job is one of these texts, for example. He suggests that the image of a just god is shaken by such texts:

that he is immoral when judged on the basis of the Old Testament doctrine of righteousness as well as modern concepts of morality — is the conclusion drawn by a number of scholars.[37]

However, the overall message of Psalms appears to be that of justice rather than oppression. The Psalms appear to reflect on the topic of social justice, as has been argued by B. V. Malchow.[38] Psalm 10, for instance, speaks of the greedy, and Psalm 49 of the rich who are social oppressors. In the face of social inequality it is God who must act:

Although the psalms say little about human assistance for the deprived, they mention divine help more than any other topic in the area of social justice.[39]

In new cases of social suffering and violence the psalmist appeals confidently to the deity for aid since the name of the Lord of Israel is already associated with the topic of justice and redemption. This movement of accepting a traditional image of God, of adapting it and transforming it to meet new social crises, is, says Malchow, a major lesson which modern readers can take from the Hebrew Bible.[40]

W. Brueggemann takes a similar line in his work on the pastoral use of psalms. In *Abiding Astonishment*[41] he investigates the image of God as a source of wonders. He argues that the historical psalms reflect an image of God who is the Wonderworker. His acts in history, which have a focus in the release of Israel from Egypt, reveal a god who enacts justice and righteousness through the everyday history of a people. This is the ideology of the historical psalms. Brueggemann suggests that modern readers have lost this image because of modernity. The methods of modern scientific thought have led scholars to dissect the texts in question with regard to modern ideas of documentary history. Thus, for instance, one can argue for the truth of the text which states that God fed his people in the desert by recourse to information about the flight patterns of birds in the area. The effect of such discourse is to marginalize the message of the Psalms. Scientific history becomes secular history and theological history is mere primitive credulity.

For Brueggemann, however, there is more to be said. In the Psalms, 'History begins in miracle. History begins in an event of "abiding astonishment".'[42] The point of this kind of history is that it can transform the reader's expectations. There is hope of further unexpected shifts and changes. Thus theological history is subversive of the status quo. Brueggemann argues that the Psalms can be viewed as texts of protest:

- the world protested against in these psalms is a one-generational world which rejects the relevance of the past for its own time
- which is devoid of authoritative covenanting, rejecting responsibility for its own actions
- which is morally indifferent
- which is monologically closed, which looks for nothing new, nothing to disturb the establishment
- which is politically indifferent[43]

He believes that the Psalms can function as political texts which call the reader to evaluate the existing structures of world society, to critique them in the light of their relationship to theological history, to offer an image of God as source of just government and of rearrangement of systems as part of righteousness in action.

In his book *The Psalms and the Life of Faith*[44] Brueggemann adds to this line of approach a focus on the centrality of God. The Psalms focus on the figure of the deity. Brueggemann finds this attitude reflected in the modern thinker, M. Buber, who discusses the existence of the 'Other', the 'You' that makes sense of the term 'I'. Brueggemann finds the parallel to this modern idea in the approach of the psalmist who constantly sets human experience in the context of a transcendent God in order to find meaning and purpose for human actions. The 'You' addressed in the OT is a figure defined by a limited but significant vocabulary:

Israel has only a few things to say about this peculiar You ... The words recur: 'righteousness', 'faithfulness', 'steadfast love', ... To these are added ... 'uprightness', 'salvation', 'peace', 'justice', and 'covenant'.[45]

With this limited semantic field the psalmist creates a theology of relatedness. God is defined as the upholder of the key terms in relation to those who turn to him. God is first the giver of meaning to the concepts described above; human content of this language field is derived from its divine significance. Once again Brueggemann describes the OT attitude of abiding astonishment at the divine achievements in the world. In this setting the image of a god of power and justice is one which frees human brings to hope for better life chances, to believe that the present order is not fixed and unchangeable, to look for moments of transformation. The effect on human attitudes of a reading of Psalm 109, for example, could be a new vision of society:

The split in much of our thinking between religion, on the one hand, and political, economic and juridical processes on the other hand, is dangerous and destructive. It results in a faith that is finally irrelevant to the great issues of the day.[46]

It is clear that the image of the god of power and justice has a range of meanings and theological possibilities, from the mythological under-standing of a deity in ancient Syro-Palestine to the foundations of modern pastoral care within the Christian community to a message of hope and empowerment for all readers of the Psalms whatever their background. At the heart of all these interpretations of the texts is the acceptance of the view that there is another dimension of existence beyond the particular human individual or human society and that there is a bridge between the individual reality here and now and that wider reality of the other. The OT describes this concept in practical terms, a God who is 'in the heavens' yet stoops down to look at what is happening 'on earth' and who reaches out to interact with earthly affairs by means of attributes which channel divine power to renew creation.

Summary

The topic of God's outreach to the world leads into a variety of means by which that outreach takes place. God can operate through wisdom, word, spirit, name, oath ... All of these are channels by which divine power and authority control events. Ultimately God is viewed as a rational being whose power is not exercised at random. Relevant resource material for these matters are found in the book of Psalms which constantly reflects on the nature of God in relation to human experience. A major image here is that of God the king. 'Justice' is a term for a proper exercise of power and the chapter investigates possibilities for the exercise of divine power. A number of modern scholars find this material useful for pastoral concerns connected with ongoing human social relations.

Notes

1   These are the complementary activities of wisdom or reason, of word or speech and of spirit or life force. Together they indicate a deity who is internally coherent and who can shape external reality via that cohesion within the self. This manner of describing God was taken further in Christian thought which saw in it the basics of a Trinitarian approach to the godhead.

2   A number of psalms refer especially to the divine Name as a means of reaching the deity. Thus, for instance, Psalms 115, 113, 105, 54, 145.

3   R. Murray discusses the theme of God's cosmic oath in *Cosmic Covenant* (London: Sheed & Ward, 1992). The book of *Enoch* refers to such an oath which God swore in relation to the founding of a nation as his people. See here Psalms 110, 132.

4   A major development of psalm research in the twentieth century has been the movement from treating these texts as pure literature to envisioning them as the record of an active liturgy. This worship setting is the real origin of psalms and shapes their meaning. Since the original shrines where psalms were performed have long since disappeared, scholars have to recreate such settings via speculation from the remaining evidence, that is, the texts. It is generally argued that the temples at Jerusalem were major cultic sites which have influenced the psalm tradition which has been inherited by modern readers. Key scholars in this shift of interpretation were H. Gunkel and S. Mowinckel.

5   Gunkel thought of each psalm as the record of a single event in the life of a community. However, some psalms had similar structures and could be grouped together. This led to a scheme of psalm classification in which the two main literary types were lament and praise. Although later scholars have altered the details of Gunkel's scheme, it remains a basic tool for modern psalm research.

6   See notes 4 and 5 above.

7   S. Mowinckel, *The Psalms in Israel's Worship* (Oxford: Blackwell, 1962).

8   J. C. McCann Jr, *A Theological Introduction to the Book of Psalms* (Nashville: Abingdon, 1993).

9   McCann (1993), p. 150.

10   McCann (1993), p. 150.

11   McCann (1993), p. 155.

12   McCann (1993), pp. 17–18.
13   McCann (1993), p. 18.
14   J. Day, *Psalms* (Sheffield: Sheffield Academic Press, 1992).
15   The suggestion here is that the Lord of Israel exists in a polytheistic religious context, as ruler and judge of other deities. This is consonant with much of the research done in the twentieth century on comparative ancient religion and the development of an overview of Syro-Palestinian religions. Mythology concerning the Lord of Israel has been referred to in a number of chapters in this book and should be viewed as the system of religious ideas which undergirds many of the OT texts.
16   Day (1992), p. 126.
17   Day (1992), p. 124.
18   M. Z. Brettler, *God Is King: Understanding an Israelite Metaphor* (Sheffield: Sheffield Academic Press, 1989).
19   Brettler (1989), p. 26.
20   Brettler (1989), pp. 32ff.
21   See note 8.
22   McCann (1993), p. 43.
23   McCann (1993), p. 48.
24   J. L. Mays, *The Lord Reigns* (Louisville: John Knox, 1994).
25   Mays (1994), p. 7.
26   Mays (1994), p. 7.
27   Mays (1994), pp. 17–20.
28   Mays (1994), pp. 20–1.
29   This is a formal device of rhetorical structure of a text. It is not that the psalmist is clearly innocent in a legal sense so much as the attitude of innocence being a prerequisite for a petitioner of the deity.
30   Mays (1994), p. 31.
31   Mays (1994), p. 32.
32   M. L. Brown, *Israel's Divine Healer* (Carlisle: Paternoster, 1995).
33   Brown (1995), p. 124.
34   Brown (1995), p. 137.
35   The topic of 'enemies' in psalm literature has long been debated. Presumably the text would have referred to real enemies such as foreign nations or opponents in a legal battle or unfriendly neighbours, but the life-setting of the actual enemies is no longer accessible to the reader. Within the language of psalms 'enemies' as a term has a formal role to play, indicating the psalmist's need for protection against the troubles which afflict human existence. The term focuses the petition for divine aid on human incapacity to solve human dilemmas.
36   R. N. Whybray, 'The immorality of God: reflections on some passages in Genesis, Job, Exodus and Numbers', *Journal for the Study of the Old Testament* 72 (1996), pp. 89–120.
37   Whybray (1996), p. 111.
38   B. V. Malchow, *Social Justice in the Hebrew Bible* (Collegeville, MN: Liturgical Press, 1996).
39   Malchow (1996), p. 55.
40   Malchow (1996), p. 78.
41   W. Brueggemann, *Abiding Astonishment: Psalms, Modernity and the Making of History* (Louisville: John Knox, 1991).

42 Brueggemann (1991), p. 31.
43 Brueggemann (1991), pp. 26–7.
44 W. Brueggemann, *The Psalms and the Life of Faith* (Minneapolis: Augsburg Fortress, 1995).
45 Brueggemann (1995), p. 44.
46 Brueggemann (1995), p. 279.

11 *The god of time in Daniel*

The book of Daniel is one of the later works in the Writings section of the Hebrew Scriptures. The first six chapters of the book present the story of a pious Jew at the Babylonian and Persian courts in the period of the Exile[1] while the later chapters offer, in coded format, a commentary on the history of Judah in the second century BCE.[2] A reader of the work may feel more comfortable with the stories about the hero Daniel of which the first six chapters are composed than with the visions of the latter part of the book but, in fact, both parts deal with the same topic, that of the nature of world affairs.

In Daniel rulers, peoples and deity operate on a cosmic scale and what is at issue is the source of power in the universe and the extent to which the destinies of secular rulers are controlled by forces outside of their own political authority. Chapter 7 provides the hinge of the book with a scene of bestowal of heavenly authority on one 'like a son of man' (7:13f.). Although this is a scene which deals with power in heaven it is connected with the issue of earthly power. The beasts from the sea which Daniel sees earlier in the same vision represent various earthly kingdoms, all of them destined to perish. By contrast, divine authority over the universe is eternal. This chapter is to be compared with the stories of Daniel, where kings are led to acknowledge the power of the Lord of Israel, and with the visions in which Daniel comes to realize that the fate of Judah is in the hands of the deity and his supernatural agents.

The chief character, Daniel, holds together the two parts of the work by acting as a focus for the presence of God in daily affairs. In the stories, for instance, Daniel's good health is maintained by divine power and not by the food of secular kings (Dan 1). Similarly, Daniel's powers of divination are in direct parallel with the divinations of the servants of the king, but Daniel's skills far transcend those of his competitors. Compare the exclamation of the foreign royal diviners in Daniel 2:10:

'There is no one earth who can reveal what the king commands!' with that of the confidence of Daniel's response to the king in verses 27–28:

No wise men, enchanters, magicians, or diviners can show to the king the mystery that the king is asking, but there is a God in heaven who reveals mysteries and he has disclosed to King Nebuchadnezzar what will happen at the end of days.

Daniel can interpret the royal dream when the local diviners fail and so the authority of the Lord of Israel is illustrated through the qualities of his human servant.

In the visionary sequence Daniel acts as a mediator of true knowledge about God to others. He is a kind of heavenly journalist, someone in the right place and time to hear and see what the supernatural beings who are the real source of action in history are up to. He can report heavenly scenes and give accounts of interviews between himself and authoritative commentators as to the meaning of what he sees. In chapter 8, for example, the initial visionary sequence, various animals appear and fight with one another and with heavenly powers — the 'host of heaven' (verse 9). Daniel is there to record what happens but he is uncertain as to its meaning. However, a heavenly figure explains to him the inner significance of the animals, which has to do with the conflict between human rulers and the rise of great kings. Daniel acts here as an interpreter of historical events who gives history its value from a heavenly perspective. The sequence in chapter 8 is parallel with the dreams and their interpretation which were the content of many of the scenes in the earlier chapters of Daniel. The climax of Daniel's role as mediator of information comes in chapter 10, where he is told that he is entrusted with the news of future events; an angel reports that he has 'come to help you [Daniel] understand what is to happen to your people at the end of days' (verse 14). Through these literary patterns, then, Daniel acts as a commentator on the power of this world's rulers.

Within this material a key topic is that of time. The question is often raised as to when some particular event will occur. Thus in Daniel 8:13, in the vision of the animals, a voice is heard asking 'For how long is this vision ... ?' And a reply is given: 'For two thousand three hundred evenings and mornings.'

This conversation is one indication of the book's overall concern with issues of time, a subject which runs throughout the text and takes several forms. One aspect of time is that of human measurement of time sequence. This tool is used in Daniel to set events into context. Chapter 1 opens with a dating of events by the reigns of great kings and this motif is repeated in later chapters. The implication of regnal dating is that world affairs are organized and controlled by human rulers. But this view is constantly challenged within the book. In 2:21, for instance, Daniel praises God for his control of affairs. He removes kings and sets up kings. He changes times and seasons. Daniel himself is evidence of God's time control, since he is given power to divine the meaning of heavenly messages given to the king in 2:29. These concern what would be hereafter, what is to be, and their content is kingdoms and their span of existence. The effect of Daniel's divinatory power is that kings are led to acknowledge that the Most High God has an everlasting kingdom and that his dominion is from generation to generation.

Part of the divine ordering of time is the special usage which God makes of units of time. Thus in the dream of the ox eating grass the king will be transformed 'till seven times pass over him' (4:23). This schematic use of the word 'time' occurs in the visions. The reader's attention has already been drawn to 8:14 where number is used to illustrate divine shaping of historical events. In chapter 9 Jeremiah's reference to 70 weeks of years as the timespan of judgement on Jerusalem is given new meaning by subdivision of that fixed time into smaller units, each of which denotes a particular stage of Judah's history following Babylonian invasion. The ultimate dimension of this supernatural view of time is represented by Belshazzar's dream in chapter 5. God is the sole arbiter of when human power comes to its close: 'God has numbered the days of your kingdom and brought it to an end' (v. 26).

The length of human rule contrasts with that of divine authority. Chapter 7 speaks of an 'Ancient of Days', a chief deity whose power has been of long duration, who bestows his authority on another supernatural being:

to him was given dominion and glory and kingship, that all peoples, nations, and languages should serve him. His dominion is an everlasting dominion ... (v. 14)

The book of Daniel, then, contains yet another image of God in the OT, that of a god of time. The deity can be identified, it seems with the sequence of events in the world and with the length and duration of any one stage of those events. Especially, the deity is connected with the moment of the passing away of any given event, with the 'End'. The vision sequence in Daniel highlights this development of thought in the book. Daniel 8:17 identifies the vision as 'for the time of the end'. Daniel 10:14 involves Daniel in learning 'what shall befall your people in the latter days'. The last chapters of the book focus on this Latter Time of the End. The End here envisaged is the collapse of Judah's enemy and the passing of final judgement on human conduct of affairs by heavenly rule:

Many of those who sleep in the dust of the earth shall awake, some to everlasting life, and some to shame and everlasting contempt. (Dan 12:2)

Even this Endtime is to be reckoned out by the concept of number, though. How long, asks Daniel, till this happens? Three answers are given — a time, two times and a half time; 1,290 days; and 1,335 days. Thus time as continuous event is interwoven with the cessation of time's movement and both are placed under heavenly authority.

The subject of time is connected with that of 'history'; history is the record of a succession of events over a period of time. In history temporal events gain a new significance when they are viewed in relation to one another — as cause and effect, for example. Daniel is both concerned with the subject of history and also is written to address the historical needs of Jews in the Persian and Hellenistic periods,[3] as P. R. Davies states in his commentary on Daniel:

Half of the book was originally addressed to Jews who were exiled, but living actually or potentially fruitful lives in Gentile domains ... The other half ... was written for a nation for whom the Gentile world had broken destructively into its own life and land ...[4].

Davies argues that the reader encounters in Daniel the god of history. This deity knows all that happens in the world and controls it all. God is supremely in charge of time[5] and intervenes in the procession of temporal affairs in order to rescue his people. Rescue comes quickly in the stories, to Daniel and his companions, but it is delayed in the visions until a dimly perceived resolution of power struggles in Judah and its environs. Thus it seems that the writer of the book was more sure of divine control of events in a previous century than in the future time which his community was facing: 'If the visions look for God at the end of history — because they do not find him in the present? — the stories look for God in the everyday.'[6]

In this context it is not just Jewish time which the deity controls but also that of the foreign nations. This dual control is established, in the stories, through the images of Jewish hero and Gentile monarch.[7] The text implies that it is possible for Jews to live peacefully under the temporal rule of Gentile empires. However there are some tensions; the kings may fail to acknowledge their subordinate position and this may lead them to harass the pious Jew who is loyal to the God of Israel. This in turn brings judgement on their authority to rule, an end to their power. In the visions this sequence of events is emphasized; the failure of Hellenistic rulers to recognize the true nature of world power and their increased hostility to Jews comes to a climax in the angel Michael's account of the coming last days of bitter warfare in heaven and on earth. Davies argues that, like Ezekiel 38 – 39, Daniel focuses on Israel's foes: 'all Israel's military humiliations are concentrated into a single epic moment when God will destroy the foe'.[8]

Davies interprets the theme of time here as indicating the climax of all passing times in one single time measurement, the time of judgement. This involves the God of Israel passing sentence on his people's enemies.

This in turn links the question of time to that of theodicy or the righteousness of God: 'the stories in Daniel affirm the righteous sovereignty of God, yet in a context where the individual Jew could not expect complete freedom from persecution'.[9]

Davies suggests that the text makes one major move in this matter of the date for the vindication of the Jews. Chapter 12 appears to pass beyond the historical measurement of time to a cosmic perspective in which time and history are themselves judged in relation to the *Eschaton* or End:

> in its final chapter [the book] passes beyond all political or national categories, and speculates ... on the transcendence of the whole order of history and nature, affirming, however allusively, that divine justice and sovereignty will be asserted, even beyond the limits of human experience and imagination.[10]

The book of Daniel deals with the subject of time, history and judgement in language which is often strange for a modern reader. In the stories there is the image of the statue symbolizing world order and in the visions the same topic is addressed in the image of the beasts from the sea, for instance. Moreover, treating dreams and visions as messages from the world beyond is itself an unusual, rather than an everyday, subject for discussion in the modern world. Language which is somewhat similar to this is found in parts of Ezekiel and Isaiah, and, outside the OT, in numerous works which the ancient world called 'Apocalypses'. From this evidence scholars have derived the term 'apocalyptic' to describe the literary style typical of such works.[11] Is the god of time, then, an apocalyptic figure?

It has to be asked, first, what is the content of this term 'apocalyptic'? K. Koch's attempt to establish criteria for the term is generally considered a classic treatment, even though scholarship has moved on.[12] Koch listed the features of apocalyptic as

- discourse cycles between the seer and his heavenly counterpart
- spiritual turmoils on the seer's part, including trance and loss of speech
- parenetic exhortation offered by the seer as a result of his visions
- pseudonymy, that is, a later writer remaining anonymous and assuming the character of an earlier great figure in Jewish tradition such as Enoch
- language which takes on a concealed meaning by means of mythical images rich in symbolism
- texts which have a composite character stemming from a long development of their contents.[13]

Since Koch's initial writing, it has become apparent that it is easier to identify the meaning of Apocalypse than of apocalyptic. This is because there exist a number of books with that title, from the ancient world, whereas the adjectival usage of the term is the construct of modern scholarship. As P. Saatchi has recently observed, 'the word apocalyptic is a modern invention, deriving from the wish to conceptualise the field of research on the affinities between the apocalypse of John and other works of its time'.[14]

What, then, is the direct meaning of apocalypse, a translation of the Greek word *apokalupsis*? It means 'revelation'. Does this mean that the god of time is a god of revelation, and if so, what does he reveal? It is true that in the Apocalypse literature the focus is on the revelation of heavenly secrets to a human seer. As has been shown in the writing of C. Rowland, the content of what is revealed in general in apocalypses covers four areas:

- What is above the earth
- What is below it
- What has been in the past
- What will be in the future[15]

Revelation and Daniel deal with only one of these topics: what will be at the Endtime. Thus the god of apocalyptic in Daniel appears to be a deity who reveals the future destiny of historical time and of the demise of history itself, expressed from the viewpoint of Jewish interests of the second century BCE.

Modern scholars have long engaged in debate concerning the origins of apocalyptic ways of addressing life and religious tradition. In this debate Daniel occupies a basic role, since it may be considered the first signs of a new style of literature which developed in the Hellenistic and Roman periods among Jews and Christians. The book's combination of moral tales and visionary scenes may reflect a dual source within Wisdom and within Prophecy.[16] This emphasis on Daniel is the result of assuming that it is the first book in a series because it is the only apocalypse book, of the many surviving texts, which entered the canon of the Hebrew Bible. If the work does occupy a foundational role in the establishment of a new literary style in Hebrew religious tradition, the image of the god of time contained in the text is, at the same time, given a high profile.

But what is the scope of the term 'time' when it occurs in Daniel as part of heavenly revealed knowledge? J. J. Collins defined the underlying issue as the contrast between life and death, with the emphasis placed on the transcendence of death. The book, he writes, 'suggests that the just can be elevated to the heavenly sphere of life to join the angelic host'.[17]

The promise of elevation comes in temporal sequence at a future time and involves the raising of the dead. In line with this approach Collins points to similar thought in the material from Qumran where the transcendence is already achieved in the community's life without having to await future historical events.[18] In this setting Collins speaks of apocalyptic eschatology, revealed knowledge about the end of history and its ultimate goal:

The apocalyptic writings had no one literally intended portrayal of the manner in which the elevation to the higher form of life will take place. Daniel speaks of a resurrection ... The Qumran community experienced the transition as a present reality, but also expected a future vindication.[19]

A further question which arises is the source from which the writer of Daniel, and those of other apocalyptic works, drew the metaphors with which to discuss their concerns over time and divine control of events. In a collection of international papers on Apocalypses[20] published recently J. H. Charlesworth[21] argues for the relevance of folk images. Symbolic imagery could be at the root of some of the depictions of heavenly beings in Apocalypses. He focuses on the image of winged deity to be found in a number of artefacts from the ancient Near East stemming from different cultures[22] and concludes that popular iconography may have made a significant contribution to descriptions of heavenly worlds:

the search for the origin of the apocalypses ... must be attuned ... to the motifs in folklore, and the symbolic consciousness of the ancient near east.[23]

The manner in which the book of Daniel clothes its image of a god of time, the figure of the 'Ancient of Days' in chapter 7, for instance, may reflect ancient mythological images which have been redeveloped to give current historical affairs their true value.

In a similar manner information concerning the range of images available for an apocalypse text can be gained from a study of comparative religion. A. Hultgard argues that the image of the metallic statue referred to in Daniel can be explored through the *Bahman Yasht*, a text from Zoroastrian religion.[24] There is a clear similarity in the two books with regard to this image. Working from this link may enable scholars to trace the development of eschatological imagery in the ancient Near East, in ancient Iranian mythology and in Hellenistic-Parthian apocalyptic.[25] This process of interpretation would locate Daniel more accurately in terms of its relationship to other Apocalypses and situate its image of a god of time in a broader context of the use of the concept of divine control of world order in comparative literature.

Scholarly interest remains focused, however, on the basic topic of identifying apocalyptic thought in early Jewish tradition, as P. Saatchi's recent work shows.[26] Saatchi takes as the oldest relevant text not Daniel, but *1 Enoch*, the *Book of the Watchers*. He regards Daniel as a later work in the series of apocalyptic thought, one which reflects Enochic themes but which has also moved on: 'With Daniel apocalyptic becomes historical, or at least alongside a decidedly cosmic apocalyptic a historical apocalyptic is born.'[27] Here Saatchi implies that it is this particular book which invents the image of a god of revealed time. Historical time is paired with spiritual or heavenly time in such a way that the meaning of the word 'time' is shifted from a this-world perspective to that of the deity. God may intervene from time to time in human affairs but this is symptomatic of a deeper reality, that time itself is dependent on God. Time is here part of the created order and will come to an end together with that same order. Time is linked with the divine plans for the cosmos, part of the hidden knowledge revealed to privileged seers:

the good world of the spirit is not to be found above the person, and already present in some way; rather the contrary: it is placed at the end of this history and it will be reached by the particular action and intervention of God.[28]

Saatchi's approach situates Daniel in a line of development of Jewish religious thought from the third century BCE onwards, but changes the position of the book from start to somewhere in the middle, the key element here being the Danielic invention of the concept of resurrection.[29]

Saatchi's interpretation of apocalyptic traditions uses as an interpretative tool the theme of the problem of evil. The *Book of the Watchers*, for example, recounts how fallen angels brought evil into the world and points to God's judgement given against them and their descendants on that account. Saatchi argues that this line of thought is a model for later apocalyptic: 'I am convinced that the centre of apocalyptic thought should be sought in the conception of sin and not in eschatology or messianism.'[30] Placing Daniel in this scheme of thought makes it clear that the work has moved away from the original pattern, for it does not know of angelic sin although it does view human society as degenerating. It is not that God had to deal with the problem of supernatural evil from the very beginnings of time, so much as that the progress of time has itself been gradually corrupted, leading the deity to pass judgement on the temporal process itself.

In later apocalypses such as the *Enochic Book of Parables* God deals with the evil of fallen angels and of their descendants through a Son of Man figure who takes the offensive against the long-term consequences of angelic corruption. Saatchi considers the Son of Man in Daniel 7 to be a forerunner of this image. He is a symbol for the people, the saints of God, whereas the later version relates to a single person, a messiah or anointed one in his own right:

He will cast down the kings from their thrones, will break the teeth of sinners ... It is he who will carry out the Great Judgement and will condemn the evildoers.[31]

Here the image of the god of time is a complex one composed of paired divine beings. God from the beginning keeps watch on temporal events and on human history but he has devolved the task of carrying out his ultimate plans to another supernatural being. In Daniel this dual image is made up of the 'ancient of Days' and the 'One like a Son of Man'.

The topic of the problem of evil and the means to deal with it bring together the reality of everyday experience on the ancient reader's part and a mythological code of explanation of these life events. Since the god of time tends to convict historical world powers of being evil the message of an Apocalypse seems to be that there is a distance between Us and Them. In Daniel this is a perspective of the Hellenistic rulers of second-century BCE Judah. In other words, the god of time is a political deity who is a major political force in history. The god of time stands up for the marginalized or oppressed in society; in Daniel this entails supporting the cause of Jewish national independence, as can be seen from the speech of the angel Michael in chapter 11.

A further question which arises, therefore, about the image of the god of time is, to whom did this image speak, for whom did it have meaning? It has frequently been argued that apocalypses were written by people at the margins of their society who had ceased to hope for the resolution of their political and social needs in their own time and so turned to an eschatological approach to life. This could easily be the source of the image of the god of time in Daniel, with its background of controversy over superpower colonial regimes.[32]

Recently, however, S. Cook has challenged this belief.[33] He draws on a wide range of sociological and anthropological research to argue that groups at the centre of local power in a region could still develop apocalypse imagery. Cook presumes that interpreting the meaning of Apocalypses starts with the matter of world-view:

Worldviews are ... created by groups ... If the mythic and bizarre language and beliefs of biblical and related apocalyptic writings are to be explained ... they must be related to a social setting with a millennial worldview.[34]

Cook then proceeds to define millennial views with reference to many actual examples of millennialist groups taken from European history and from the culture of groups such as the North American Indians, and of Jainism. From this evidence he comes to the conclusion that millennial groups which look for a future intervention by the god(s) to restore good fortune and power to their members may sometimes be persons at the centre of an existing culture rather than those who exist at the margins.

If this theory is applied to Daniel it offers the possibility that the book is not written out of the despair of a minority, outlawed group within Hellenistic Judah but by groups at the centre of local affairs. It would then express the positive hopes of a resilient society which looked forward to the time when the region's superpowers would be finished and its own political and economic strengths could emerge. This would fit with the latter part of the second century BCE when the Maccabean revolt led to the independent Hasmonean state run by Jewish priest-kings. The god of time, in this setting, is concerned less with the overall end of all history and more with the end of regional history as it had developed over a number of centuries. Eschatology would thus be concerned with a new stage of history, a new era of time such as is referred to in chapter 11 of Daniel, a time when the wars of God's people would be over.

Cook's treatment of apocalyptic emphasizes the real history of everyday politics in a given period as against that of the mythology in which the message is expressed. It remains true, however, that the god of revealed time is a mythological figure in terms of the imagery used to convey this image. This area of mythology and its significance for situating created time in relation to the divine has been explored by N. Cohn.[35]

Cohn surveys a number of ancient mythologies concerning the creation of the cosmos out of chaos, drawn from ancient Egypt, Mesopotamia, Israel, Persia and India. Daniel can be situated in this context since the ancient mythological imagery of the Near East which tells of divine victory over chaos represented as water and as strange beasts is found in Daniel and forms an integral part of the message of the book:

In the beasts emerging from the ... sea [chaos monsters] rise to new life ... Like those primordial beings, the pagan empires war against the divinely appointed order.[36]

In Cohn's research cultural anthropology throws new light on the long debate among scholars concerning apocalyptic imagery. Cohn argues that it issues ultimately from a common strand of human culture, that of a mythology of time and history. These concepts take their value from myths of origins in which creation and chaos compete for control of the universe. Any particular time or ruler can be measured against the underlying mythology and an opinion given as to the weight to be placed on current historical events. It is this activity which is at the root of a book like Daniel.

The impact of this approach is that it gives the reader of Apocalypses a sense of purpose and design about the world. Chaos is matched by creation, hope balances despair. P. R. Davies, however, in *Whose Bible Is It Anyway?*,[37] argues that the old mythological certainties have given way in Daniel to a new and despairing position. Whereas the stories show a High God in control even of great kings, the visions reveal a world handed over to lesser divine beings who cannot resolve its tensions or foresee an actual end to evil and oppression.

Daniel is addressed by a series of angels but not by God directly, and when he enquires anxiously in chapter 12 about the length of time before events come to their climax he is told to go away and die ('take rest') and stop asking difficult questions. The interpretive key which Davies picks out is chapter 7 of the book where an old god hands over to a supernatural being who is not of the same rank. What Daniel was seeing was effectively the death of God:

Elyon is no longer directing history. He is effectively dead ... To Daniel his successors can offer promises ... but these ... betray confusion and lack of direction, and hint at incompetence in world management.[38]

In this interpretation a truly innovative approach to apocalyptic world-views is outlined, one in which God is marginalized and the world of time and history meanders on aimlessly. The determined enthusiasm of the marginal group waiting for rescue, or the secure belief of a core élite in the power of its deity and the value of its cult, or the unifying value of an underlying thought-pattern in the culture of a region, are set aside. Time and deity are both relativized. The god of time is revealed as a powerless old man, dreaming of past victories while his younger counterparts struggle to control a world order which continually slips through their grasp.

This approach to the god of time in Daniel is at the opposite pole to the view that the image of the deity in this work is concerned with control of events, a control tightly held and exercised through supernatural servants. Davies's views express a possible readership of elders who have for long experienced the uncertainties of life and consequently do not believe in divine intervention. The views of Cook, for instance, offer the alternative — a group of elders at the centre of power who expect divine support for their cause. This approach is more clearly seen in second Isaiah where the divine title of First and Last states incontrovertibly God's authority over time. Imaging the God of the OT as a god of time, then, has more than one message to offer the modern reader.

Summary

The final chapter on Writings turns to a book with an individual identity in the OT, the book of Daniel. This is said by modern commentators to be an apocalypse and the chapter explores the meanings of that term. Daniel is ultimately concerned with one issue, that of time and events within the frame of time. The image of God here is of a being in charge of history. Such a presentation again raises questions about power —

this time the power of world empires compared with divine power. Is the God of Daniel greater than world powers and is this a source of optimism for the reader, or is Daniel unsure as to the final outcome of history?

Notes

1 'The Exile' is a biblical term which describes the invasion of Judah by Babylonia and its effects. The royal family and other leading figures were deported to Babylonia and Judah became part of the Babylonian Empire, passing to Persian control when the Babylonian dynasty died out. A major issue for deported Judaeans (Jews) was how to maintain their ancestral faith while living in an alien culture. The books of Tobit and Esther reflect this need to work out a viable lifestyle when living outside the homeland.

2 Judah passed from Persian to Greek hands with the victories of Alexander the Great and then became part of the Hellenistic Empire administered by Alexander's generals and their dynasties. Judah came under the influence of the Seleucids of Syria until the rebellion led by the Maccabees. More information about this period can be had from reading the first two books of Maccabees.

3 P. R. Davies gives an introduction to the historical background of the work at the beginning of his commentary on Daniel.

4 P. R. Davies, *Daniel* (Sheffield: Sheffield Academic Press, 1985), p. 81.

5 Davies (1985), p. 86.

6 Davies (1985), p. 87.

7 Davies (1985), ch. 7.

8 Davies (1985), p. 97.

9 Davies (1985), p. 119.

10 Davies (1985), p. 120.

11 For an account of the basic material connected with apocalypticism see e.g. J. J. Collins, 'Old Testament apocalypticism and eschatology' in R. Brown, J. Fitzmyer and R. Murphy (eds), *The New Jerome Biblical Commentary* (Englewood Cliffs, NJ: Prentice-Hall / London: Geoffrey Chapman, 1989).

12 K. Koch, 'What is apocalyptic? An attempt at a preliminary definition' in P. D. Hanson (ed.), *Visionaries and Their Apocalypses* (London: SPCK, 1983).

13 Koch (1983), pp. 20–4.

14 P. Saatchi, *Jewish Apocalyptic and Its History* (Sheffield: Sheffield Academic Press, 1990), p. 26.

15 C. Rowland, *The Open Heaven* (London: SPCK, 1982).

16 Scholars are divided as to whether apocalyptic is a late form of prophecy or a development from the wisdom tradition of the OT. See here P. D. Hanson, 'Old Testament Apocalyptic re-examined', *Interpretation* 25 (1971), pp. 454–79, and Davies (1985), ch. 10.

17 J. J. Collins, 'Apocalyptic eschatology as the transcendence of death' in Hanson (ed.) (1983) p. 71.

18 Collins (1983), p. 72.

19 Collins (1983), p. 76.

20 J. J. Collins and J. H. Charlesworth (eds), *Mysteries and Revelations: Apocalyptic Studies since the Uppsala Colloquium* (Sheffield: Sheffield Academic Press, 1991).

21 J. H. Charlesworth, 'Folk traditions in Jewish apocalyptic literature' in Collins and Charlesworth (eds) (1991).

22 Charlesworth (1991), pp. 103 ff.

23 Charlesworth (1991), p. 110.

24 A. Hultgard, *'Bahman Yasht*: a Persian apocalypse' in Collins and Charlesworth (eds) (1991).

25 Hultgard (1991), p. 134.

26 Saatchi (1990), p. 26.

27 Saatchi (1990), p. 67.

28 Saatchi (1990), p. 85.

29 Saatchi (1990), p. 104.

30 Saatchi (1990), p. 113.

31 Saatchi (1990), p. 166.

32 For information concerning Jewish groups in this period see L. Grabbe, *Judaism from Cyrus to Hadrian* (London: SCM Press, 1994).

33 S. L. Cook, *Prophecy and Apocalypticism* (Minneapolis: Augsburg Fortress, 1995).

34 Cook (1995), p. 26.

35 N. Cohn, *Cosmos, Chaos and the World to Come* (New Haven: Yale University Press, 1993).

36 Cohn (1993), p. 170.

37 P. R. Davies, *Whose Bible Is It Anyway?* (Sheffield: Sheffield Academic Press, 1995).

38 Davies (1995), p. 136.

12 Moving to a close: God and us

Towards the start of this book the point was made that the approach to be followed was that of exploring the many and various images of God in the OT, taking them each separately and so providing a tapestry of pictures of the divine. That is the method which has been carried through in the main sections of the text. Now the time has come to round off this exploration of the meaning of the term 'God' in the OT. It would be possible, at this stage, to attempt to harmonize the different images by submitting them to the control of one overriding principle of interpretation, but that would be to subvert the procedure followed in the earlier chapters. Instead the present investigation will come back to the basic images of God to be found in Genesis 1 – 11, a subject explored in Chapter 2 of this work.

These images consisted of three elements — God the creator, the judge and the redeemer. These three roles of God were shown to provide an ideological perspective for the rest of the OT. It is now appropriate to return to these theological foundations, not directly to find out more about God, but rather to consider the total content of those images in order to return finally to concepts of the deity. For each of the three modes of divine operation automatically involves a partnership or relationship. To be a creator means that one is linked to that which is created; to be a judge requires that which is judged; to be a redeemer involves the redeemed. In each case, in Genesis, it is human beings who form the other half of the image of the divine. The texts reveal the faces of a God known through his connections with humankind. To explore the deity means, in this instance, to investigate the nature of human existence — the created, judged and redeemed human beings from whose perspective the OT is written.

This study begins with the concept of 'the created'. God is known to us human beings at all because he wanted to be known, because he decided to create the world to be filled with human beings who, like their creator, could bring forth life in their turn. Miles comments on this creative act in his biography of God: 'God makes a world because he wants mankind, and he wants mankind because he wants an image.'[1]

Miles surmises the divine reasons for this desire and points out that the God of the OT is alone in the heavens before he enters into a timeless relationship with the work of his own hands:

He seems to be entirely alone ... His life is about to become hopelessly entangled with the determination of his image to make images of its own. But if God's life lacked human entanglements, what kind of life would it be?[2]

Human beings are thus entirely dependent on the creator but at the same time the deity is himself shaped and conditioned by his own creative act.

The human species has a mixed nature: Adam is created from *adamah*, earthling from the earth. But this being is animated by the divine *ruach* (breath or spirit) which God breathes into the lifeless shape. One part of human existence is tied closely to creation. Genesis 2 tells the reader that the earth waited incomplete until God created the worker who was one with it and whose labour would bring it to completion in organized productivity. But the other part of human identity is more elevated and also more perilous. 'Let us make Adam in our own image' says the God of Genesis 1 – 2 and so it came about. As the deity rules the heavens so humankind rules the earth on God's behalf (Gen 1). The subdivision of Adam into *ish/issah* offers further information. Humans can be defined as husband (*ish*) and as wife (*issah*), as man and woman. This complementarity within the species may also be an image of the divine since God says 'Let us make ...'.

These realities of human life give greater complexity to the image of a god of creation. God is about rule and relationship and both are tied up with human beings. Humans can be divine icons, mirrors of the deity. As C. Westermann has argued in his study of the origins of Wisdom material in the OT, this understanding of the divine–human alliance leads human readers of the text to an attitude of praise:

It is the Creator who has so wonderfully created the human being. One's awe-filled consideration of the handiwork of the human body with its organs and senses has the repercussion of praise for the creator ...[3]

At the same time, however, Wisdom reflection on divine creativity provides a boundary to human life. Genesis 3ff. explores the collapse of the original intimacy between God and creature; Wisdom texts which turn on the phrase 'But YHWH ...' have a parallel intention:

It is the work of the Creator that defines the limits of human potential. Created by God, the human finds his limitations manifest in his mortality and fallibility.[4]

This boundary involves the addition to the deity of the role of judge of human affairs.

Genesis 3 reflects on the quality of human wisdom. The opportunity offered to humans there is to capitalize on their existing intellect in order to become equal with the deity (Gen 3:5). The power to know good and evil represents power to control their own destiny, but the seizing of the chance to obtain that power brings not unity with God but rather a major separation — the banishment from the heavenly garden home. The image of God the judge reminds the reader of the limits of human capacity and the frustrations involved in that reality. The book of Qohelet (Ecclesiastes) carries a similar sense of the nearness, and yet the gap, between God and humans. In chapter 3 the Preacher reflects on the fact that God has put the concept of *olam* (eternity) into the human brain, but so that human beings may not attain the reality of such time. There is a mysteriousness about the deity in this context since God withdraws from human comprehension. The alternative to mystery here is tyranny; God deliberately taunts humans with knowledge of a precious thing which cannot ever be attained. Ecclesiastes and Job both verge at times on asserting that the meaningless of life reflects an arbitrary, coincidental side to the deity. However, the OT traditions in general contain this thought within the image of divine sovereignty:

this is the basis for the fear of God: the eternity and the enormous power of 'the God' contrasted with the impotence and the ephemerality of the human ... the tragedy for humans is that God does not reveal to them the direction of cosmos and history ... Humans fear what they cannot understand, yet has the power to control their lives.[5]

The image of the divine judge is connected, then, with the theme of human ignorance. Such ignorance leads to inappropriate action which in turn unties the world order created by God. The divine perspective on this subject is that it comprises sinfulness, whether human sin, as in Genesis 1 – 11, or angelic sin which leads human beings astray, as in the book of *Enoch* (the watchers). In the Wisdom tradition of the OT this underlying image of the judging God is the basis for the categorization of human nature which constitutes the instructive purpose of the writers:

The antithesis of the righteous and the wicked surfaces with profound acuteness in the proverbs that are inclusive of the operation of God and one's relationship to God. At the same time that the power of Yahweh is a refuge for the righteous, it is ruin for the wicked.[6]

Despite the sense of justice involved in this version of God the judge, giving back good for good and bad for bad, the image retains a sense of the ominous for the reader of the OT: 'the creator has proven to us that he has the capacity to be a destroyer'.[7] God the judge gives way to the redeeming deity, one who rescues Noah from the Flood and returns creation to its original design for life and fertility. The very name, Noah, gives the reader a feeling of security since it means 'rest'. In this new beginning there is renewed hope for the return of intimacy between God and us. Yet nothing is quite the same:

Despite the rainbow, the Lord God cannot now cease to be an object of fear as well as admiration ... he remains a permanently threatening presence.[8]

This is Miles's summary of the God of these earlier chapters of the OT. It reflects the presence in the text of a new emphasis. The relation between God and humans now takes on a new formality, involving a structured commitment on both sides. God promises Noah that he will not break out into total destruction, but will make an everlasting covenant with his descendants (Gen 9:8–17). Noah has already demonstrated the correct human contribution to such a covenant by the offering of worship and sacrifice to God. The God of redemption can be relied on to support human beings, but only while their response acknowledges the gap between deity and servant. A great suzerain supports a lesser king in return for loyal service. Human beings are in the image of God but they are definitely not divine beings as such. God rules alone in the heavens.

The concept of God as a redeemer who offers covenant to humans can, however, be viewed as opening up positive aspects as well as negative ones. Brueggemann views this image as the basis for effective pastoral care:

The primary claim of 'covenant' as a way of understanding our theme of pastoral counselling and theological anthropology is that human persons are grounded in Another who initiates personhood and who stays bound to persons in loyal ways for their well being.[9]

This Other is not a remote and faceless principle of goodness but rather 'a quite specific, identifiable God whose name we have been told and into whose history we have been invited'.[10] This deity is one who calls into being, who remains caring of creation and who redefines human existence. Thus biblical theology establishes some foundations for anthropology:

The God of this covenant relation is one who is understood not as the passive, silent upholder, but as an active agent on our behalf. Pastoral care involves bringing persons to such a knowledge of self in the presence of God.[11]

In this statement Brueggemann defines human identity as derived from a knowledge of God. This could be turned around — it is possible to identify God through knowledge of the human condition. It has been the argument of this chapter that the images of God as creator, judge and redeemer operate in that fashion. In order to know what the exact content of each of these titles is, it is necessary to turn to human experience of being created, judged and redeemed.

Perdue summarizes the analysis of human experience offered by Ecclesiastes as centred on the theme of death:

Solomon teaches a somber and sobering lesson from the tomb: All is breath that quickly vanishes ... The ephemerality of human existence and human accomplishments is made worse by the innate desire to retain the life-giving spirit that comes from God, but only for a passing moment.[12]

It is within this chilly but realistic context that the deity is to be situated:

Humanity is not the center of reality, nor are humans the measure of all things. God, not humanity, rules over creation and directs history, though in utter secrecy. The temporal character of human existence is contrasted to the eternity of God and the cosmos.[13]

This can be viewed as the ultimate message conveyed to the reader through texts which examine humanity in relation to God. Comfort in life turns on acceptance of divine sovereignty, that is, on taking on board an image of God defined as superior to us. Genesis 1 – 11 reflects the gradual unfolding of this image, according to Miles. God in his solitary state does not know who he is; it is only as the interaction between deity and humans develops that God discovers his own depths.

God, as the Bible begins, is as yet unmade by any history and is therefore less than evident to himself. Though he is, uniquely, a protagonist who gives life itself to his antagonist, he is also, uniquely again, a protagonist who receives his life story from his antagonist.[14]

This approach to God in the OT gives rise to a further aspect of the human–divine interaction. If God were indeed writing his own story would it have the present shape of the OT? Who, among humans, can answer that question? For the story of God in the OT is the human story of God; it is the deity as seen by human experience expressed in order to give meaning to that same experience. Human wisdom and human images mediate the figure of a universal deity to human readers in human language.

Notes

1   J. Miles, *God: A Biography* (New York: Simon & Schuster, 1995), p. 28.
2   Miles (1995), p. 29.
3   C. Westermann, *The Roots of Wisdom* (Edinburgh: T. & T. Clark, 1995), p. 125.
4   Westermann (1995), pp. 125–6.
5   L. Perdue, *Wisdom and Creation: The Theology of Wisdom Literature* (Nashville: Abingdon, 1994), p. 218.
6   Westermann (1995), p. 128.
7   Miles (1995), p. 46.

8   Miles (1995), p. 46.
9   W. Brueggemann, *The Psalms and the Life of Faith* (Minneapolis: Augsburg Fortress, 1995), p. 151.
10   Brueggemann (1995), p. 151.
11   Brueggemann (1995), p. 157.
12   Perdue (1994), p. 238.
13   Perdue (1994), p. 242.
14   Miles (1995), p. 89.

13 Conclusion: God, the Old Testament and godtalk

In the last chapter it was pointed out that the OT images of God are shaped by human experience of life and by human language structures. The OT, it could be said, represents human beings talking to human beings about God. To make this point is not to say anything about the divine inspiration of the Christian Bible; it simply reflects the reality of literature as a human communication channel. The sacred books of world religions are used by communities of faith to explore and to found their own identity as worshippers of the divine. The present study is an investigation into the religious ideas to be found in the OT texts and, as such, does not intend to deal directly with issues of faith.

The language of the OT is human language, emerging out of particular cultures and time periods, expressing views on God. One category of such language is that of mythology. Mythological vocabulary and concepts are at the root of some central OT images of God such as the god of law and covenant, the god of the Temple, the god of apocalypse. The frequency of such language in the OT argues for its popularity in its own cultural setting. However, modern readers from the culture of the industrial West would mostly be bewildered by such imagery and easily led to discard it as marginally relevant for understanding the images of God in the OT. This illustrates the difficulty inherent in assuming that biblical language is easily accessible to any possible reader, ancient or modern, and that it conveys a single understanding of the deity to every reader.

Language is, then, one of the basic issues for the study of biblical texts — the nature and appropriate use of religious language by human beings. Just as the language of a text is culture-bound so is the perspective of any given reader. She or he belongs to one particular cultural setting and, whether or not this is consciously realized, reads text automatically from the viewpoint of that membership. Modern scholars have labelled this culture-linked reading, ideology. The ideology of writers and readers of the OT is indeed the subtitle of a recent scholarly study of biblical exegesis.[1] Language and ideology, then, are the topics of this concluding chapter.

Ideology represents the kind of spectacles which the human being puts on to read text, the lenses through which a reader views the OT. There is no single content to the term 'ideology' since each reader brings his or her personal ideology to the task of searching for a text's meaning. In recent years there has been a heated debate among biblical scholars as to the weight to be given to these separate ideologies. In particular a clash has arisen between those who consciously operate from a base in Christian faith communities and those who wish to speak primarily from an academic base in university departments.

A study by P. R. Davies examines this topic.[2] Davies fights for the acceptance of a non-Christian, post-Enlightenment ideological perspective which he defines by the term 'Academy' and which is contrasted with another perspective defined as 'Church':

there are three arenas of bible study. One is the church, which, as a confessing community, requires its Bible for devotional and liturgical purposes; ... A second arena is the 'biblical studies' of the academy, which is humanistic and non-confessional ... A third is 'Scripture' which is the subdiscipline of theology that deals with 'the Bible'. This discipline exists *physically* within the domain of the academy but serves the church, or claims to.[3]

Davies argues that, although the interests of church and academy are not inherently opposed to each other, being simply different objectives, there often exists a confusion over the methods of interpreting Scripture since the interests of the church can take over this area to the exclusion of the legitimate interpretive concerns of the academy.

In a later chapter Davies applies his basic 'ideology' to sections of OT text. He states that the subject of god(s) in the OT can only be studied appropriately from the content of the literature itself:

From an *etic* [i.e. objective] point of view, 'god/gods' can *only* be approached in such a way, that is as constructions within a publicly accessible communication.[4]

In addition the authors who produced these texts

like virtually every other human being in the ancient Mediterranean world ... believed in deities, however few or many, and that they were telling stories ... about categories of being that they believed in.[5]

The ideology offered here is that any reading must be individual-text based while acknowledging the importance of the topic of God to the original writer. This basis should not lead, according to Davies, to any creation by the reader of texts of a global OT religion. The texts cannot deliver a system of beliefs, a 'religion' nor a 'theology' beyond the confines of the stories themselves, since stories create their own worlds.[6]

Davies then examines some of the narratives of Genesis 1 – 11, with a view to the god to be found there. Initial reading of text allows the detailed subsections of the chapters to appear. Biblical scholars have long agreed that there are clearly two distinct accounts of God as creator in the first two chapters of the book, in the first of which God is Elohim and in the second YHWH (Elohim). The personality of these two 'gods' is distinct since the first is shown as a disembodied voice of command whereas the second has hands, since he can form dust into a human shape, or take a rib out of Adam's side. But the same attitude to a creator god appears in both accounts, that of a benevolent deity concerned with the human species. This must feed the reader's interpretation of the text. But, according to Davies, more than one line of interpretation can arise from this:

Those who read Genesis 2–3 apart from ch. 1 will be tempted to see in it a story of human disobedience and punishment ... with humans ... the originators of sin ... However, reading Genesis 1 and Genesis 2 together shows that the disobedience and the punishment are actually *mechanisms for fulfilling the divine intentions in creating humans*.[7]

YHWH punishes humans but in sending them forth from the garden fulfils the purpose for which they were created by his alter ego, Elohim. This alters one's view of Eve. Reading A leaves Eve/women to carry the can for all human disasters in the universe whereas Reading B shows Eve as the free, rational human being using her god-given powers to interact with the environment and so to fulfil Elohim's plans.[8] Davies contrasts two ideologies, that typical of the Christian church and the other which he suggests from his own perspective within the academy. The effect of these separate interpretations of OT text is the distinguishing of two 'gods' and the collapsing of the view that there is a systematic treatment of a single deity in the OT.

The views of Davies have been hotly contested by those who feel that their ideologies are being unfairly represented as exclusive of the opinions of other readers. Among critics of Davies is F. Watson, whose 1996 article[9] is designed as a response to Davies's book. Watson describes Davies's ideology as targeting

the view of the Bible as primarily 'the book of the Christian community' — a view which is (he thinks) especially pernicious when it filters through into the world of academic biblical scholarship.[10]

Watson argues that this approach sets up a rigid boundary between insider and outsider attitudes to the Bible. The insider is the church member using text for resourcing worship and belief. Such a person has no place in the academy which, in turn, is the habitat of the outsider, someone who studies the Bible as another piece of world literature. The attempt of insiders to operate their ideological approach to the Bible from within the academy has led to confusion of interpretation and is to be deplored. It is this version of the state of biblical scholarship which Watson contests. He points out that Davies talks of the value of pluralism, of allowing different ideologies to co-exist within the academy, while, to Watson's view, denying his own claims in reality through his exclusion of a Christian ideology as a valid interpretive framework.

Watson, too, has an ideological stance which he wishes to make known:

But what if ... one denies that the text is a neutral site and that the choice of perspective is a matter of indifference, asserting instead that the holy Scriptures ... are to be understood in the light of their manifold yet single testimony to the action and being of the triune God disclosed in Jesus ... ?[11]

Watson is clearly advocating a boldly Christian ideology here. Such an ideology has its own shape and purpose. These can be defined, but they cannot be abandoned for a shapeless pluralism of a supposedly neutral character. Nor is the Christian ideology only for the church; rather it takes its place alongside other 'scientific' modes of thought within the biblical studies of the academy:

A christian theological interpretative practice cannot do otherwise than claim that it alone can accommodate itself to the true reality of these texts in their constitutive relation to the history of divine self-disclosure which has brought them into being.[12]

As one ideology among others in the academy the Christian mode of reading text would enter into genuine dialogue with other, separately-composed ideological positions.

The question of ideology is broader in scope than a contemporary contest between two scholars. A recent edition of the journal *Currents in Research* carried an article which gives a wide survey of the subject.[13] Pippin points out that all readers have ideologies:

I tell the fundamentalist Christian students in my introductory Bible classes that if we gathered a roomful of so-called biblical inerrantists, there probably would not be one singular interpretive agreement on any biblical passage.[14]

Such readerly ideologies are often linked with issues in everyday affairs such as power and wealth matters. Thus the ideology of reading often means a 'political agenda'. Reading a text for what it offers on the situations of the marginalized or oppressed is such an ideology, whether the conclusion is that the status quo should remain or should be shattered.

The background to the term 'ideology' can be traced since the 1790s, including its use by Marx to denote the oppressive world-view of the upper classes by which they control the masses. Here it is text which has ideology, reflecting as it does the value-system of the author. In the present time interpreters of the ideological tendency of text may prefer a deconstructionist approach to one which explores the formal structure of a book whereby a single message emerges from the literature. For instance, for T. Eagleton the book of Jonah is not about unity but about chaos: 'God is a spineless liberal given to hollow authoritarian threats, who would never have the guts to perform what he promises' (Eagleton, p. 231).[15] The possibility of multiple meanings to be drawn from a single text leads to instability. D. Jobling, for instance, thinks that 'texts are unstable; therefore meaning is unstable but connected to a web of social political and economic relations'.[16] This implies that there is some focus for the meaning of texts but that focus is itself complex and multi-valent, drawn as it is from the complexities of a given societal context within which it emerged.

What is the impact of ideological exegesis on concepts of God in the OT? The example given above relating to the God of Jonah yields the possibility that the term 'God' itself becomes unstable, dependent for content not only on different books but on different sections of a single text. This was clear in the account of the God of Genesis 1 – 11 given by Davies, referred to above. In Chapter 7 of this book reference was made to the critique made by feminist writers of the term 'God' in the OT. For some feminist scholars such as E. Schüssler Fiorenza, the term 'God' is so unstable that it is 'under erasure' as unsuitable for conveying an authentic message to the reader concerning the transcendent level of the universe.

But can the ideology of the text be differentiated from the ideology of the reader? Some, such as S. Fowl,[17] would argue that texts do not have ideologies. They are innocent of intent. Thus even texts of oppression and violence are redeemable. In this context the warrior God of Deuteronomy would be capable of being installed centre-stage in the exploration of images of an OT God. 'Hermeneutics', the reader's principles of interpretation, take over from the term 'ideology' here. It is these tools of the trade which make or break a text. Liberationist readings represent one manner of hermeneutic through which any given text may be read; this reading in turn illustrates the nature of the liberationist hermeneutic in its own right. All hermeneutical styles are equal, though historically, according to Pippin, the First World, male, model has had precedence in biblical studies. There is a need to resist this dominance:

The hegemony of traditional scholarship in Europe and the United States is becoming decentred in a postmodern, postcolonial world where meaning is fragmented. One of the dangers ... is that First World biblical scholarship may re-inscribe colonization by co-opting the readings of the marginalized.[18]

In this matter of ideology, then, the term 'God' acquires another broad range of meanings. As well as images conveyed by an ancient text to an original audience there are the ideologies used by all the generations of readers in their times and places. 'God' is thus an umbrella term for many separate and often opposing interpretations of the relevance of the divine for human beings.

It could be argued that that is not so bad since, in any case, the phrase 'images of God' refers to metaphorical use of language which is itself imprecise. Here is a link between ideology and language; God in a Christian theological approach is a term with clear content, but the biblical God is often hidden. This contrast led R. P. Carroll to write of God the hidden problematic:

theology operates with abstract philosophical notions, whereas much of the language of the Bible is highly metaphorical. In philosophical talk, God is abstract ... In biblical language, God is a character in a narrative, a player in a story.[19]

Whereas theology wishes to create a god of philosophy, capable of being described in a systematic and coherent manner, the biblical writers pick up and discard metaphors of God, loosely modelling their character on an Oriental potentate:

Immensely powerful, generally all-knowing and much given to outbursts of temper, this being manipulates humans and regularly intervenes in situations in order to achieve certain ends.[20]

Within this frame God acts and speaks in ways which, when closely scrutinized, may be contradictory. But metaphor and image are more difficult to align with the concept of contradiction than are logical statements and propositions and so evade attempts to pin them down to single meanings. One of the OT metaphors for God, that of a hidden deity, indeed makes nonsense of the systematic Christian ideology of God as always defined by revelation, according to Carroll. Such a hidden deity appears in the OT in Psalms, for example. When the psalmist laments his fate and appeals to God to save him he is experiencing a silent and absent deity:

the metaphor of divine hiding combines all the anthropomorphic language of the Bible. It represents a god who has face and eyes and whose social mores reflect an emperor or king's gestures of averting or turning the face to the petitioner.[21]

In the broader context the image of a hidden god is combined with one who appears and comes so that revelation is itself determined by its opposite. But this does not make for a straightforward systematic code of language about the God of the OT. Instead, it offers the reader meaning through contradiction and difference.

Metaphor itself is, of course, the subject of scholarly research. J. Martin Soskice, for instance, addresses this matter in her book on metaphor and religious language.[22] Religious language, discourse about God in human terms, is itself both true and untrue. True insofar as it manages appropriately to convey ideas about the divine in its own right in concepts developed in a different level of existence: untrue because such discourse is always at one remove from its proposed topic.

Within this broad comment on the value of religious language there is a place for the discussion of the particular role of metaphor. Images in the OT appear to arise from a variety of human experiences, 'Amos's personification of Israel as a young woman, Hosea's depiction of God as a compassionate herdsman'.[23] But, Soskice argues, these images have been deliberately chosen to describe the deity and are evidence of a notion that no one image is sufficient to describe a God of Being (YHWH). In this process a metaphor is known to be both a real and an unreal conveyor of meaning. The Christian image of Christ as Lamb of God is unreal since Jesus is not a young sheep as such. But the OT tradition had attached certain meanings to 'lamb' which had religious significance and which can be said to impute a real value to the term when it is used as a christological title.

This balance between the image in its own right and its meaning in a transfer of language situation extends from single phrases to larger text units such as parables. In a parable a metaphor is extended into a story which in turn gives meaning to the term God. But is God in fact an unjust judge, for instance? In terms of a complete identification between either a human being and a god or between unjust judgement and the justice of God there is clearly incomplete transference of meaning. But is the parable, then, a very clumsy and inexact attempt to convey the identity of God? The point of using a parable at all, though, is that it does bring deity and reader face to face in the activity of reading. It would be possible to view this encounter as reader encountering character in text, however, and not as reader meeting with a god who exists both within and objectively outside the text. Such a use of religious language would have some further consequences:

This radical but consistent alternative would involve the redefinition, perhaps along existentialist lines, of central concepts like 'truth' and 'reality', and even of 'god' and 'man'.[24]

On a different, but not unrelated topic, that of how to define the word 'God' in its own right, it might be possible to rise above the difficulties of biblical metaphorical language and produce some commonly agreed logical statement: 'A striking attempt at such is Anselm's formula in the Proslogion, "God is that than which nothing greater can be conceived".'[25] However, on examination, Anselm's statement says nothing about God *per se*. God is defined only in contradistinction to the importance of other things. God, as Being, may not be capable of being conceived at all and so God as a concept stands outside the world in which language operates to convey meaning from writer to reader.

By contrast with these complexities of logical, abstract thought the biblical, metaphorical God is often more accessible to the reader who knows the substance of terms such as judge, king, parent. But the problem of such language remains. Particular imagery may go out of date, especially mythological imagery, and some images may convey to the reader ideas which were probably not consciously intended by the ancient writer. And so the topic of images of God in the OT leads the student of biblical texts into a variety of tasks which are, at first sight, not obviously central to biblical research. Among these is the requirement to be aware of the possibilities and also of the constraints of human language. Considerations of language lead to the topic of literature as a form of human communication and this in turn raises the issue of the social context within which particular language arises, how language reflects society's values. Nor is it a matter only of the social context of biblical language in the ancient world; attention needs to be given to the social context of the language which a modern reader of the OT uses in order to describe biblical meaning.

Notes

1   D. Clines, *Interested Parties: The Ideology of Writers and Readers of the Hebrew Bible* (Sheffield: Sheffield Academic Press, 1995).

2   P. R. Davies, *Whose Bible Is It Anyway?* (Sheffield: Sheffield Academic Press, 1995).

3   Davies (1995), p. 24.

4   Davies (1995), p. 81.

5   Davies (1995), p. 81.

6   Davies (1995), p. 82.

7   Davies (1995), p. 88.

8   Davies (1995), pp. 88–94.

9   F. Watson, 'Bible, theology and the university: a response to Philip Davies', *Journal for the Study of the Old Testament* 71 (1996), pp. 3–16.

10   Watson (1996), p. 3.

11   Watson (1996), p. 11.

12   Watson (1996), p. 13.

13   T. Pippin, 'Ideology, ideological criticism and the Bible', *Currents in Research: Biblical Studies* 4 (1996).

14   Pippin (1996), p. 51.

15   Pippin (1996), p. 55.

16   Pippin (1996), p. 57.

17   Pippin (1996), p. 58.

18   Pippin (1996), p. 60.

19   R. P. Carroll, *Wolf in the Sheepfold* (London: SCM Press, 1997), p. 37.

20 Carroll (1997), p. 37.
21 Carroll (1997), p. 55.
22 J. Martin Soskice, *Metaphor and Religious Language* (Oxford: Clarendon Press, 1985).
23 Soskice (1985), p. 77.
24 Soskice (1985), p. 106.
25 Soskice (1985), p. 138.

Postscript

This study of images of God in the OT set out to examine the variety of modes, within the OT, by which information about the deity, YHWH, is conveyed. It has continually offered the reader yet another image to set alongside the previous one. And this process has lasted to the final page of the main text. The writer has preferred to leave the reader with a tapestry, or even a patchwork quilt, of divine figurations rather than to end by subordinating the variety to one common theme.

It may be that the reader is unsure, finally, of the meaning to be placed on this material. But that is because there is no one fixed meaning to be found. Each reader may have a favourite image from among those presented here — or may prefer an image which the present study has not explored. Each reader will probably put a different evaluation on the individual issues current in scholarship.

The present book, then, is an opportunity for the reader of the OT to explore the range of possible meanings and messages of that collection of texts, to engage in reflection on the deeper levels of textual content, and to come to some personal conclusions, for the time being, as to the significance of this literature in the contemporary world. It provides a tool and, it is hoped, an enthusiasm, for further research and development for the student engaged in biblical studies.

Bibliography

A. Alt, *Essays in Old Testament History and Religion* (Oxford: Blackwell, 1966).

K. Baltzer, *The Covenant Formulary* (Oxford: Blackwell, 1971).

M. Barker, *The Gate of Heaven* (London: SPCK, 1991).

M. Barker, *The Great Angel* (London: SPCK, 1992).

J. B. Bauer (ed.), *Encyclopaedia of Biblical Theology* (London: Sheed & Ward, 4th edn 1982).

A. Brenner, *The Israelite Woman: Social Role and Literary Type* (The Biblical Seminar 2; Sheffield: Sheffield Academic Press, 1994).

M. Z. Brettler, *God Is King: Understanding an Israelite Metaphor* (JSOT Supplement Series 76; Sheffield: Sheffield Academic Press, 1989).

M. L. Brown, *Israel's Divine Healer* (Carlisle: Paternoster, 1995).

W. Brueggemann, *Abiding Astonishment: Psalms, Modernity and the Making of History* (Louisville: John Knox, 1991).

W. Brueggemann, *The Psalms and the Life of Faith* (Minneapolis: Augsburg Fortress, 1995).

R. P. Carroll, *Wolf in the Sheepfold* (London: SCM Press, 1997).

J. H. Charlesworth (ed.) *The Old Testament Pseudepigrapha*, vols 1–2 (London: Darton, Longman & Todd / New York: Doubleday, 1983, 1985).

J. H. Charlesworth, 'Folk traditions in Jewish apocalyptic literature' in J. J. Collins and J. H. Charlesworth (eds), *Mysteries and Revelations: Apocalyptic Studies Since the Uppsala Colloquium* (Sheffield: Sheffield Academic Press, 1991).

B. V. Childs, *Old Testament Theology in a Canonical Context* (London: SCM Press, 1985 / Philadelphia: Fortress, 1986).

J. Chittister, *WomanStrength* (London: Sheed & Ward, 1990).

R. E. Clements, *Deuteronomy* (Sheffield: Sheffield Academic Press, 1989).

R. Clifford, 'Exodus' in R. Brown, J. Fitzmyer and R. Murphy (eds), *The New Jerome Biblical Commentary* (Englewood Cliffs, NJ: Prentice-Hall / London: Geoffrey Chapman, 1989).

D. J. Clines, *Interested Parties: The Ideology of Writers and Readers of the Hebrew Bible* (Gender, Culture Theory Series 1; Sheffield: Sheffield Academic Press, 1995).

G. W. Coats (ed.), *Saga, Legend, Tale, Novella, Fable: Narrative Forms in Old Testament Literature* (JSOT Supplement Series 35; Sheffield: Sheffield Academic Press, 1984).

N. Cohn, *Cosmos, Chaos and the World to Come* (New Haven: Yale University Press, 1993).

J. J. Collins, 'Apocalyptic eschatology as the transcendence of death' in P. D. Hanson (ed.), *Visionaries and Their Apocalypses* (London: SPCK, 1983).

J. J. Collins, 'OT apocalypticism and eschatology' in R. Brown, J. Fitzmyer and R. Murphy (eds), *The New Jerome Biblical Commentary* (Englewood Cliffs, NJ: Prentice-Hall / London: Geoffrey Chapman, 1989).

J. J. Collins and J. H. Charlesworth (eds), *Mysteries and Revelations: Apocalyptic Studies Since the Uppsala Colloquium* (JSP Series 9; Sheffield: Sheffield Academic Press, 1991).

S. L. Cook, *Prophecy and Apocalypticism* (Minneapolis: Augsburg Fortress, 1995).

F. M. Cross, *Canaanite Myth and Hebrew Epic* (Cambridge, MA: Harvard University Press, 1973).

P. R. Davies, *Daniel* (OT Guides Series; Sheffield: Sheffield Academic Press, 1985).

P. R. Davies, *In Search of Ancient Israel* (JSOT Supplement Series 148; Sheffield: Sheffield Academic Press, 1992).

P. R. Davies, *Whose Bible Is It Anyway?* (JSOT Supplement Series 204; Sheffield: Sheffield Academic Press, 1995).

J. Day, *God's Conflict with the Dragon and the Sea* (Cambridge: Cambridge University Press, 1985).

J. Day, *Psalms* (OT Guides Series; Sheffield: Sheffield Academic Press, 1992).

J. De Moor, *The Rise of Yahwism* (Leuven: Leuven University Press, 1990).

W. Dietrich, 'The "ban" in the age of the early kings' in V. Fritz and P. R. Davies (eds), *The Origins of the Ancient Israelite States* (Sheffield: Sheffield Academic Press, 1996).

M. Douglas, 'Sacred contagion' in J. F. A. Sawyer (ed.), *Reading Leviticus: A Conversation with Mary Douglas* (Sheffield: Sheffield Academic Press, 1996).

D. Edelman (ed.), *The Triumph of Elohim* (Kampen: Kok Pharos, 1995).

M. Eliade, *Myth and Reality* (New York: Harper & Row, 1963).

J. Cheryl Exum, *Plotted, Shot and Painted: Cultural Representations of Biblical Women* (Sheffield: Sheffield Academic Press, 1996).

V. Fritz and P. R. Davies (eds), *The Origins of the Ancient Israelite States* (JSOT Supplement Series 228; Sheffield: Sheffield Academic Press, 1996).

G. Garbini, *History and Ideology in Ancient Israel* (London: SCM Press, 1988).

D. E. Gowan, *Theology in Exodus* (Louisville: John Knox, 1984).

L. Grabbe, *Judaism from Cyrus to Hadrian* (London: SCM Press, 1994).

L. K. Handy, *Among the Hosts of Heaven* (Winona Lake, IN: Eisenbrauns, 1994).

L. K. Handy, 'The appearance of pantheon in Judah' in D. Edelman (ed.), *The Triumph of Elohim* (Kampen: Kok Pharos, 1995).

P. D. Hanson, 'Old Testament Apocalyptic re-examined', *Interpretation* 25 (1971), pp. 454–79.

P. D. Hanson (ed.), *Visionaries and Their Apocalypses* (London: SPCK, 1983).

C. T. R. Hayward, *The Jewish Temple* (London: Routledge, 1996).

A. Hultgård, 'Bahman Yasht: a Persian apocalypse' in J. J. Collins and J. H. Charlesworth (eds), *Mysteries and Revelations: Apocalyptic Studies Since the Uppsala Colloquium* (Sheffield: Sheffield Academic Press, 1991).

P. Joyce, *Divine Initiative and Human Response in Ezekiel* (JSOT Supplement Series 51; Sheffield: Sheffield Academic Press, 1989).

O. Keel, *The World of Biblical Symbolism* (London: SPCK, 1978).

G. Kittel (ed.), *Theological Dictionary of the New Testament*, vols 1–10 (Grand Rapids: Eerdmans / London: SCM Press, 1964–71).

K. Koch, 'What is apocalyptic? An attempt at a preliminary definition' in P. D. Hanson (ed.), *Visionaries and Their Apocalypses* (London: SPCK, 1983).

A. L. Laffey, *Wives, Harlots and Concubines* (Philadelphia: Fortress, 1988).

N. P. Lemche, 'From patronage society to patronage society' in V. Fritz and P. R. Davies (eds), *The Origins of the Ancient Israelite States* (Sheffield: Sheffield Academic Press, 1996).

Tremper Longman III and D. G. Reid, *God Is a Warrior* (Carlisle: Paternoster, 1995).

J. C. McCann Jr, *A Theological Introduction to the Book of Psalms* (Nashville: Abingdon, 1993).

D. J. McCarthy, *Treaty and Covenant: A Study in Form in the Ancient Oriental Documents and the Old Testament* (Analecta Biblica 21; Rome, 1963).

J. G. McConville, *Law and Theology in Deuteronomy* (JSOT Supplement Series 33; Sheffield: Sheffield Academic Press, 1984).

J. G. McConville, *Grace in the End* (Carlisle: Paternoster, 1993).

J. McKeating, *Ezekiel* (OT Guides Series; Sheffield: Sheffield Academic Press, 1993).

J. L. McKenzie, 'Aspects of Old Testament thought' in R. Brown, J. Fitzmyer and R. Murphy (eds), *The New Jerome Biblical Commentary* (Englewood Cliffs, NJ: Prentice-Hall / London: Geoffrey Chapman, 1989).

J. E. McKinlay, *Gendering Wisdom the Host* (JSOT Supplement Series 216; Sheffield: Sheffield Academic Press, 1996).

B. V. Malchow, *Social Justice in the Hebrew Bible* (Collegeville, MN: Liturgical Press, 1996).

A. D. H. Mayes, 'On describing the purpose of Deuteronomy' in J. Rogerson (ed.), *The Pentateuch* (Sheffield: Sheffield Academic Press, 1996).

J. L. Mays, *The Lord Reigns* (Louisville: Westminster John Knox, 1994).

G. E. Mendenhall, 'Covenant forms in Israelite tradition', *Biblical Archaeologist* 17, (1954), pp. 50–76.

J. Metz and E. Schillebeeckx (eds), *God as Father, Concilium* 143 (Edinburgh: T. & T. Clark, 1981).

J. Miles, *God: A Biography* (New York: Simon & Schuster, 1995).

J. Milgrom, 'The changing concept of holiness in the pentateuchal codes with emphasis on Leviticus 19' in J. F. A. Sawyer (ed.), *Reading Leviticus: A Conversation with Mary Douglas* (Sheffield: Sheffield Academic Press, 1996).

A. R. Millard and D. J. Wiseman (eds), *Essays on the Patriarchal Narratives* (Leicester: Inter-Varsity Press, 1980).

M. E. Mills, *Human Agents of Cosmic Power in Hellenistic Judaism and the Synoptic Tradition* (JSNT Supplement Series 41; Sheffield: Sheffield Academic Press, 1990).

S. Mowinckel, *The Psalms in Israel's Worship* (Oxford: Blackwell, 1962).

R. Murphy, 'Introduction to wisdom literature' in R. Brown, J. Fitzmyer and R. Murphy (eds), *The New Jerome Biblical Commentary* (Englewood Cliffs, NJ: Prentice-Hall / London: Geoffrey Chapman, 1989).

R. Murray, *The Cosmic Covenant* (London: Sheed & Ward, 1992).

E. W. Nicholson, *Exodus and Sinai in History and Tradition* (Oxford: Blackwell, 1973).

J. J. Niehaus, *God at Sinai* (Carlisle: Paternoster, 1995).

M. Noth, *The History of Israel* (2nd edn; London: A. & C. Black / New York: Harper & Row, 1960).

B. Otzen, H. Gottlieb and K. Jeppesen, *Myths in the Old Testament* (London: SCM Press, 1980).

L. G. Perdue, *Wisdom and Creation: The Theology of Wisdom Literature* (Nashville: Abingdon, 1994).

T. Pippin, 'Ideology, ideological criticism and the Bible', *Currents in Research: Biblical Studies* 4 (1996).

A. C. J. Phillips, *Ancient Israel's Criminal Law* (Oxford: Blackwell, 1970).

M. H. Pope, *El in Ugaritic Texts* (Supplement to Vetus Testamentum, 1955).

J. B. Pritchard (ed.), *Ancient Near Eastern Texts Relating to the Old Testament* (Princeton: Princeton University Press, 1950; 2nd edn, 1955; 3rd edn, 1969).

R. Radford Ruether, 'The female nature of God: a problem in contemporary religious life' in J. Metz and E. Schillebeeckx (eds), *God as Father, Concilium* 143 (Edinburgh: T. & T. Clark, 1981).

J. Rogerson (ed.), *The Pentateuch* (Sheffield: Sheffield Academic Press, 1996).

C. Rowland, *The Open Heaven* (London: SPCK, 1982).

P. Saatchi, *Jewish Apocalyptic and Its History* (JSP Supplement Series 20; Sheffield: Sheffield Academic Press, 1990).

J. F. A. Sawyer (ed.), *Reading Leviticus: A Conversation with Mary Douglas* (JSOT Supplement Series 227; Sheffield: Sheffield Academic Press, 1996).

E. Schüssler Fiorenza, *Jesus, Miriam's Child, Sophia's Prophet* (London: SCM Press, 1994).

M. J. Selman, 'Comparative customs and the Patriarchal Age' in A. R. Millard and D. J. Wiseman (eds), *Essays on the Patriarchal Narratives* (Leicester: Inter-Varsity Press, 1980).

M. Smith, *The Early History of God* (New York: Harper & Row, 1990).

J. M. Soskice, *Metaphor and Religious Language* (Oxford: Clarendon Press, 1985).

Y. Spiegel, 'God the father in the fatherless society' in J. Metz and E. Schillebeeckx (eds), *God as Father, Concilium* 143 (Edinburgh: T. & T. Clark, 1981).

C. Stuhlmueller, *Creative Redemption in Deutero-Isaiah* (Analecta Biblica; Rome: Gregorian University Press, 1970).

T. L. Thompson, 'The intellectual matrix of early Biblical narrative: inclusive monotheism in Persian period Palestine' in D. Edelman (ed.), *The Triumph of Elohim* (Kampen: Kok Pharos, 1995).

T. L. Thompson, 'How Yahweh became God: Exodus 3 and 6 and the heart of the Pentateuch', *Journal for the Study of the Old Testament* 68 (1995), pp. 57–74.

P. Trible, *God and the Rhetoric of Sexuality* (London: SCM Press, 1978).

J. Van Seters, *Abraham in History and Tradition* (New Haven: Yale University Press, 1975).

P. Vardy, *The Puzzle of God* (London: HarperCollins, 1990).

G. Vermes, *The Religion of Jesus the Jew* (London: SCM Press, 1993).

G. Von Rad, *Old Testament Theology*, vols I and II (Edinburgh and London: Oliver & Boyd, 1962).

G. Von Rad, *Holy War in Ancient Israel* (Grand Rapids: Eerdmans, 1958).

F. Watson, 'Bible, theology and the university: a response to Philip Davies', *Journal for the Study of the Old Testament* 71 (1996), pp. 3–16.

M. Weinfeld, *Deuteronomy and The Deuteronomic School* (Oxford: Clarendon Press, 1972).

A. Weiser, *Introduction to the Old Testament* (London: SCM Press, 1961).

C. Westermann, *The Promises to the Patriarchs* (Philadelphia: Fortress, 1980).

C. Westermann, *Genesis 1 – 11, Genesis 12 – 36, Genesis 37 – 50* (3 vols; Minneapolis: Augsburg Fortress, 1984–86).

C. Westermann, *Genesis: A Practical Commentary* (Grand Rapids: Eerdmans, 1987).

C. Westermann, *The Roots of Wisdom* (Edinburgh: T. & T. Clark, 1995).

R. N. Whybray, *The Second Isaiah* (OT Guides Series; Sheffield: Sheffield Academic Press, 1983).

R. N. Whybray, 'The immorality of God: reflections on some passages in Genesis, Job, Exodus and Numbers', *Journal for the Study of the Old Testament* 72 (1996), pp. 89–120.

J. W. H. van Wijk-Bos, *Re-imagining God: The Case for Scriptural Diversity* (Louisville: John Knox, 1995).

Index